INTRODUCTION TO DEVELOPMENTAL PSYCHOLOGY

Genetic Foundations and Prenatal Development

INTRODUCTION TO DEVELOPMENTAL PSYCHOLOGY

Genetic Foundations and Prenatal Development

Afzalur Rahman

KALPAZ

Published by

Kalpaz Publications
C-30, Satyawati Nagar,
Delhi – 110052
Ph.: 011-47034999, 9811692060
www.kalpazpublications.com
E-mail: kalpaz@hotmail.com

Distribution Network
gyanbooks.com
India, USA, Canada, UK, Australia, France

ISBN: 978-93-5722-273-0 (HB)

First Published, 2023

Printed at: Gyan Press, Delhi.

INTRODUCTION TO DEVELOPMENTAL PSYCHOLOGY
Author: Afzalur Rahman

Foreword

The study of Developmental Psychology has become increasingly important in recent years as understanding the biological, cognitive, and environmental factors that contribute to our development is crucial in helping us to both understand our behaviour and to develop effective strategies to support growth.

This book '*Introduction to Developmental Psychology: Genetic Foundations and Prenatal Development*' is an important contribution to the field of developmental psychology. With a special focus on the genetic foundations of human development from conception to birth, this book is an invaluable resource for anyone wanting to gain a deeper understanding of the complexities of human development. From exploring the theoretical foundations and methods of developmental psychology to delving into the genetic basis of human development, this book provides an insightful overview of the subject. It also covers genetic disorders and their interventions, milestones and hazards of prenatal development, and different types of birth.

The book is a valuable resource for students, researchers, and anyone interested in understanding the fundamentals of developmental psychology, and in particular the genetic foundations of human life. It is written in an accessible and engaging style, and provides a comprehensive overview of the subject matter. I highly recommend this book to anyone who wishes to gain a better understanding of the genetic foundations of human development and the complexities of prenatal development. Enjoy the journey!

Dulumoni Goswami
Professor of Education
Gauhati University

Preface

The developmental psychology, as it today, is the upshot of the discipline 'child psychology' that itself emerged as a result of scientific investigations on children started in nineteenth century. Until then, common beliefs and practices inherited through tradition and authority were mostly used in child brought up. The emergence of an independent discipline for studying children under the heading 'child psychology' can be traced back to 1882 with the publication of a book entitled 'The Mind of the Child" (1882/1888), authored by W. Preyer, a German psychologist, which was a detailed description of the development of his own daughter from birth to two and half years. Parallel to Preyer in German, G. Stanley Hall played a significant role in establishing the discipline.

However, the 'child psychology' as it emerged in nineteenth century had mainly concentrated to study the behaviour of children. The developmentalist's at that time somehow failed to realise the dynamic nature of development; rather believed that change occurs in distinct steps or stages. Consequently, the early studies were limited to pre-school and school-age children. But, with the increase in the quantum of knowledge and theories of development, it was soon realised that change is a gradual process, and hence achievement at one stage may build on previous stage. Consequently, the interest of the developmentalists had shifted, resulting in broadening of the scope of 'child psychology' in two areas-(a) to study the pattern and process of development along with the products and (b) to study the development from prenatal to adolescence stage. Since the scope of child study was enlarged, the discipline 'child psychology' was included in the broader heading 'developmental psychology'. Thus, developmental psychology is emerged as a subject of study that investigates the products as well as process of development of human beings starting from prenatal stage to adolescence stage.

The modern developmental psychologists in the twenty-first century have started investigating the problems of old and middle age people under the jurisdiction of developmental psychology. Until recently, the developmentalists ignored the old age people due to many reasons like difficulty in finding representative samples and proper methodology etc. But, in the present century due to increased percentage of people surviving through their old ages unlike before, the importance of studying old age has been realised and a new discipline named 'gerontology' have been evolved. Similarly, the middle age people also have now come under the scientific investigation of developmental psychology. In this way the modern developmental psychology took its present shape that adopts a life-span approach in studying human development starting from conception to death.

Today, research on human development across life-span has increased greatly and is in the process of evolution. It is a common phenomenon that institutions of higher education mostly offer one or two semester courses on developmental psychology, which may be sufficient from academic point of view, but quite insufficient to get a broader perspective of human development. It is firmly believed that developmental psychology shall not be studied merely to earn some academic credits, rather to better understand life experiences of self and others, appreciate development through life, learn more about children- better interact with them, spot their problems, and help them grow and develop. Today's youths or students are tomorrow's parents, teachers, elders, and care givers. Therefore, a segmented knowledge of stages of development would fail miserably in making today's students, tomorrow's ideal parents, teachers, elders, and care givers. As such, a comprehensive study of human development covering entire ranges of human life, from the moment of conception throughout death is crucial. With this intention in mind, it is planned to prepare a comprehensive text to provide a broad overview of human development, covering a chronological portrayal of life-span development starting from conception throughout old age.

The book '*Introduction to Developmental Psychology: Genetic Foundations and Prenatal Development*' is the first edition in this attempt. The book is divided in to six chapters and encompasses a broad introduction to the field of developmental psychology, its concept, nature, scope, issues, goals, and historical background. It provides a lucid and simple description of the major theories, and methods of studying human development. The representation of human development starting from conception throughout prenatal development to birth process has been made in an orderly sequence. The description of the process of beginning of life, covering an introduction to reproductive cells, the fertilisation process- natural as well as alternative techniques, are articulated. The major focus of the book is to throw light on the genetic foundations of human life. The questions like how far genetic inheritance makes an individual unique? how far genetic inheritance determines our observable traits? how does genetic inheritance determine sex of the offspring? how does genetic inheritance contribute to multiple births? etc. are tried to explain in an eloquent approach. A synoptic sketch of different genetic disorders like Down Syndrome, Klinefelter Syndrome, XYY Syndrome, Turner Syndrome (TS), Fragile X Syndrome (FXS), Phenylketonuria (PKU), Sickle Cell Anemia, Tay-Sach Disease, Spina Bifida, Cystic Fibrosis etc. are also portrayed. Finally, the book ends with the discussion of prenatal development, its milestones, factors, hazards, and interventions. Since the birth process significantly influences the later developments in human life, a brief note on the different types of birth, their pros and cons are also included.

In a nutshell the book '*Introduction to Developmental Psychology: Genetic Foundations and Prenatal Development*' is meant not only for the students of developmental psychology, but also for the teachers, parents, prospective parents, care givers, nurses, social workers, and all others who questions how do people come to be the way they are? All attempts are tried to organise and present the contents as logically as possible in a simple language, yet no perfection is claimed in the present work.

I take this opportunity to extend my sincere gratitude to my parents, spouse, my son, my brothers, in-laws, and all those who extend their support and encouragement in accomplishing this work. My special thanks go to Professor Gayatree Goswamee, Professor Dulumoni Goswami, without whose guidance and support the work would not have been possible. My thanks go to the Principal Dr. Sarat Borkataki, Dr. Sanjay De, all the faculty members and my research scholars of the Education Department of Nowgong College (Autonomous) for their valued suggestions. I acknowledge my grateful indebtedness to all the authors, editors and publishers of the books, research papers, web pages and other forms of materials that I had consulted while writing this book.

I extend my special thanks to Kalpaz Publications, New Delhi for taking the cognizance in publishing the work into a readable text and bringing out this on time. I do look forward to any suggestions from my readers for further improvement in the next edition of the book which is likely in coming years, incorporating discussion of human development in postnatal period.

Afzalur Rahman

Contents

1

Conceptual Background of Developmental Psychology

INTRODUCTION

Psychology, as we know, is the study of behaviour. More particularly, it is concerned with the study of human behaviour in relation to their environment with an aim to make it more relevant and adaptive. In doing so, psychology includes human beings irrespective of their age, professions, mental processes, sex, culture, and environment etc. The task is gigantic since the behaviour of people of different ages, of different professions, of different mental process, of different cultures greatly differs. For example, the behaviour and developmental pattern of an infant is completely different from that of an adult. The behaviour of a criminal person is different from the behaviour of a military person. Similar conclusions can be drawn regarding other variables like mental process, culture, environment etc. Despite the differences, it becomes imperative to study the developmental pattern of human beings with all conditions and behaviour in all the dimensions. As such, psychology for its wider application have been sub-divided in to a number branches covering specific areas or fields of human behaviour like child psychology, adolescence psychology, developmental psychology, adult psychology, social psychology, educational psychology, criminal psychology, abnormal psychology, clinical psychology and so on. Thus, developmental psychology is nothing but one of the branches of psychology that deals with the product and process of development. The following paragraphs best describe the meaning and nature of developmental psychology.

WHAT IS DEVELOPMENTAL PSYCHOLOGY?

Developmental psychology, as evident from its nomenclature, is a branch of psychology that deals with development. For a layman, development means change in any attribute, entity, thing, or person. But in psychology, development implies the process through which a conceived embryo in the mother's womb turns in to a full-fledged human being passing through different stages of life. Scientists define development as the orderly and sequential changes that an individual experiences as he/she moves from conception to death. Thus, knowing what development is, it becomes easy to comprehend what developmental psychology is. It is that psychology which covers human development from conception until death. In more precise way, it can be said as a branch of psychology that seeks to understand how people change as they grow older. Since development is a systematic and orderly process, always following a pattern, developmental psychology is defined as the study of systematic continuities and changes in humans that occur from the time of conception to the time of death.

Though developmental psychology is concerned with how individual changes over time, it also considers the stability in peoples' lives. Because, developmental psychologists assume that though the process of development persists throughout every stage of human life, there is lack of uniformity in the rate of development in different dimensions of development at different stages. At some point people continue to grow and change with respect to some dimensions, while remain same in some other dimensions. Thus, developmental psychology is the science that seeks to understand the ways in which people change while remaining same in some respects as they grow older.

Human beings develop when changes occur in their body, mind, spirit, intellect, language, and social relationships. Thus, development broadly takes place essentially in three domains-physical, cognitive, emotional-social. Developmental psychology is a positive branch of psychology that incorporates all these domains of behaviour under its jurisdiction. It studies the changes occur in a person's body, its structure as well as functions; changes occur in mental activity, including sensation, perception, memory, thought, reasoning, and language; and changes occur in one's personality, emotions, and relationships with others. Thus, developmental psychology is a broad discipline that includes all the dimensions of individual's personality-cognitive, affective, and conative.

As stated earlier, developmental psychology adopts life-span approach. It studies the development covering all the stages of human life starting from conception to death. The origin of life-span approach of development is not that much old. Earlier the psychologists were interested in the study of some segments of life-span like childhood, adulthood, or old age. Infancy and adolescence were emphasised by early developmentalists as most important periods and studied under the heading 'child psychology'. Gradually with the expansion of knowledge, it is realised that the study of some segments of life-span in isolation is insufficient to get a complete picture of how and when people develop over time and the factors associated with it. Since development is a continuous process, there is a cause-and-effect relationship among various stages of life so far development is concerned. Whatever development is attained in a particular stage may be the result of interventions taken in pervious stage. Similarly, whatever is achieved or not achieved in a particular stage may in turn affect development in the later stages. Thus, there is always interrelation among the stages of life. In addition, we know that besides heredity the development is greatly influenced by environmental influences and influences from the people around him/her. The influence on a child provided by a 20-year-old mother may be of different sort from the influences provided by an experienced 40-year-old mother. So, the child development is the outgrowth consequence of adult development. In order to understand the influence on a child we need to understand the behavioural pattern of the people who exerts those influences. Based on the above assumptions the focus of developmental psychologists has shifted from infants and children to people of all ages on a life-span approach and the academic discipline 'child psychology' was included under the broader heading 'developmental psychology'.

Elizabeth B. Hurlock described developmental psychology as the branch of psychology that studies intra individual changes and inter individual changes within these intra individual changes. It describes, explains, predicts, and sometimes aims to modify age related behaviour from conception to death. 'Developmental psychology' besides describing the products of development, tries to explain the process of development with an extensive study of genetic as well as environmental influences, unlike 'child psychology' that limits itself in description of the aspects and products of development of children. Modern developmental psychologists intend to explore the underlying causes of a behaviour characteristic of a given period and try to predict and sometimes modify its consequences in future. In this context, the definition given by La Bouvie as the task of developmental psychology is 'not only description but also explication of age-related change in behaviour in terms of antecedent-consequent relationships' is worth mentioned.

In the light of the above discussion, we can draw the following conclusions regarding the meaning of developmental psychology.

1. Developmental psychology is a positive branch of the subject psychology that investigates the ways in which people change as they grow older, while remaining same in some aspects.
2. It describes, explains, predicts, and sometime aims to modify age related behaviour of people.
3. Developmental psychology, in its study of human development, covers the life-span starting from conception to death.

4. It studies the products as well as process of development by placing more emphasis on the roles played by environmental factors.

5. Developmental psychology incorporates, within its vicinity, all the domains of behaviour- cognitive, affective, and conative.

NATURE OF DEVELOPMENTAL PSYCHOLOGY

The nature of developmental psychology is almost clear while discussing its meaning as given above. In examining the nature of any academic discipline few questions come to our mind like- whether it is a science or an art? If science, what type of science is it? Whether it is a positive or normative science; an applied or a pure science? In case of developmental psychology also, the answers to all these questions would help in comprehending its nature in a more precise way. In this connection following points may be summarised.

1. There is no disagreement to the fact that developmental psychology is a science, since it came in to being from the scientific study of human development. In its process of investigation, developmental psychology adopts scientific methods and techniques like any other sciences.

2. Developmental psychology is a positive science, not a normative science. A normative science concerns with 'what ought to be', while a positive science studies 'facts as they are'. Developmental psychology intends to study the behaviour characteristics of all ages as they are, with an aim to predict and modify future development through adopting scientific procedures. It does not set norms as what behaviour characteristic should be, which is the concern of normative sciences like axiology, ethics etc.

3. Though developmental psychology is called a positive science, it cannot claim exact validity and reliability as claimed by other positive sciences like physics, chemistry

etc. Because, the subject matter of developmental psychology is human being which is less reliable and more variable. However, since it adopts scientific procedures in studying human behaviour, it is better to call it a positive science.

4. Developmental psychology possesses both applied as well pure aspect. The primary concern of any applied science is the application of scientific knowledge, theories, and principles, whereas the generation of new knowledge or theories is its secondary concern. On the other hand, the primary objective of any pure or fundamental science is generation of new knowledge, theories, and principles, whereas their application is its secondary objective. Developmental psychology performs both the task with some magnitude. It borrows the well organised theories possessed by the subject psychology as well as undertakes research of its own to develop new theories for the study of human development.

5. Modern developmentalists examine the behaviour characteristics of people of all ages starting from conception to death. Hence, developmental psychology is a life-span approach.

EMERGENCE OF DEVELOPMENTAL PSYCHOLOGY

The developmental psychology, as it today, is the upshot of the discipline 'child psychology' that itself emerged as a result of scientific investigations on children started in 19th century. The advent of industrial revolution in 19th century brought with it an increasing demand of factory workers having basic literacy and numeracy skills. This demand for literate workers was met by making primary education compulsory. Eventually, it became important to undertake scientific investigations to study children's behaviour so that the education system could be made effective and efficient. Other factors like hygiene, disease control, increased wealth etc. had given impetus to scientific study on children.

Until 17th century the researchers were not interested in studying children in their child nature, despite recognising early childhood as a distinct period in the life cycle. Since the children were considered as miniature adults, the researchers were concentrated to study adults and tried to apply the findings on children as investigating adults was much easier than investigating children. John Amos Comenius, the famous Slavic educational reformer of the 17th century, was one of the first persons who realised the need of studying children as a distinct individual and not as a miniature adult. Comenius was of the view that in order to understand the capacities of children and to deal effectively with them, children should be studied in their essential child nature, not as embryonic adults. Following the view of Comenius, some advancement was made in child study during 18th century. Pestalozzi published the first scientific record of the development of a young child in the year 1774 based on the observational notes of his 3 and half year-old son. Later, psychologists like Tiedemann of Germany, Millicent Shinn of America have contributed in the study of young children by publishing biographical notes of development of young children based on their own observations. Simultaneously in 18th century, educational reformers started contributing in the development of the field by generating philosophical treatises on education in which children were studied indirectly. Popular among them were John Locke and Jean Jacques Rousseau. Rousseau, in the mid of 18th century had described three stages of development- infancy, childhood and adolescence in his book 'Emile', which were strongly taken up by educators of that time.

However, studies on children in more scientific way (based on actual observation of developing children) were started in the second half of the 19th century, when Charles Darwin had published a short paper based on the detailed observation on the development of his own infant son, Doddy, in 1877, for which he is often credited with introducing first scientific methods to the study of development. Darwin's studies on his infant son were intended to understand the evolution of innate forms of human communication. Our present understanding that development is the result of progressive adaptation of the child to his/her environment, can be traced directly to the influence of evolutionary theory of Darwin. Darwin's theory was vigorously popularised by psychologists in the later part of the 19th century.

The emergence of an independent discipline for studying children under the heading 'child psychology' can be traced back to 1882 with the publication of a book entitled 'The Mind of the Child" (1882/1888), authored by W. Preyer, a German psychologist, which was a detailed description of the development of his own daughter from birth to two and half years. Parallel to Preyer in German, G. Stanley Hall played a significant role in establishing the discipline across the USA. In 1891 Hall had come up with his work "Concepts of Children's Minds on Entering School" that had given new impetus to child study movement. Stanley Hall was strongly influenced by the evolutionary theory of Darwin and as such he tried to correlate the ages of childhood with previous ages of mankind. He advocated recapitulationary aspect of human development and was of the view that human development involves a repetition of the ancestral, evolutionary time-table. However, Hall's views were criticised by many psychologists at that time. Psychologists argued that Hall's recapitulationary aspect of development lacks systematic programme of thought. The idea of repetition of the ancestry, for example, mistakenly bound us to accept the fact that a child loves to swing in trees because he recapitulates his monkey ancestry. However, except the recapitulationary aspect, Hall's comparative observations on child development were of great interest providing significant and reliable inputs to the field. Moreover, he was the person who had founded the Pedagogical Seminary in 1891 in USA. He was an importer and translator of research in child development and worked hard in theorising that was being carried out beyond the USA. He helped to bring Preyer's book, 'The Mind of the Child' to a wider audience in America. Soon, many psychologists and educators became interested in studying children and thousands of studies of almost all phases of child development have started appearing. Subsequently, an organised discipline had emerged and was known as 'child psychology'. Since, it was G. Stanley

Hall who popularised child study as an important area of scientific investigation by stimulating interests of researchers, he is often referred as the 'father of child study movement'.

However, the 'child psychology' as it emerged in 19th century was mainly concentrated to study the behaviour of children. The developmentalists at that time somehow failed to realise the dynamic nature of development, rather believed that change occurs in distinct steps or stages. Consequently, the early studies were limited to pre-school and school-age children. Moreover, emphasis was given on investigating certain aspects and products of development, giving little or no importance on the pattern and process of development. But, with the increase in the quantum of knowledge and theories of development, it was soon realised that change is a gradual process, and hence achievement at one stage may build on previous stage. It was also realised that merely identifying the aspects or products of development would not add to the understanding of how behavioural characteristics changes as children grow older and what causes such changes. Consequently, the interest of the developmentalists had shifted, resulting in broadening of the scope of 'child psychology' in two areas- (a) interest was given to study the pattern and process of development along with the products and (b) interest was given to study the development from prenatal to adolescence stage. Since the scope of child study was enlarged, the discipline 'child psychology' was included in the broader heading 'developmental psychology'. Thus, developmental psychology is emerged as a subject of study that investigates the products as well as process of development of human beings starting from prenatal stage to adolescence stage by giving more importance on environmental influences. James Mark Baldwin (1861-1994), Sigmund Freud (1856 -1939), Jean Piaget (1896 -1980), Lev Semionovich Vygotsky (1896 -1934), John Bowlby (1907 - 1990) and J. B. Watson (1878 – 1958) were among the popular psychologists who had contributed maximum in the emergence of modern developmental psychology with their extensive theories on human development. The Psycho analytic theory of Freud, Baldwin's stepwise theory of cognitive development and Theory of Mind (ToM), Piaget's theory of cognitive development, Vygotsky's theory on influence of culture on child development, Bowlby's theory of emotional development and formation of personality and Watson's theory of behaviourism have significant bearing in the emergence of developmental psychology as a definite academic discipline and indeed much of the current researches in developmental psychology are influenced by these theories.

The modern developmental psychologists in the 21st century have started investigating the problems of old and middle age people under the jurisdiction of developmental psychology. Until recently, the developmentalists ignored the old age people due to many reasons like difficulty in finding representative samples and proper methodology etc. But in the present century,due to increased percentage of people surviving through their old ages unlike before, the importance of studying old age has been realised and a new discipline named 'gerontology' have been evolved. The word 'gerontology is derived from the Greek word 'geron' meaning 'old man' and 'ology' meaning 'the study of'. It is concerned with all facets of ageing. Similarly, the middle age people also have now come under the scientific investigation of developmental psychology. In this way the modern developmental psychology took its present shape that adopts a life-span approach in studying human development starting from conception to death.

CHILD PSYCHOLOGY VERSUS DEVELOPMENTAL PSYCHOLOGY

A detailed comprehension of the facts and discussions made under the sections- nature and emergence of developmental psychology presented earlier, gives a picture of the basic differences between 'child psychology' and 'developmental psychology'. However, to make it more precise for the readers, the following points of difference between two are given.

1. The scope of child psychology is narrow than the scope of developmental psychology. Developmental psychology encompasses a broader area of investigation in comparison

to child psychology in two ways. It goes deep in studying the developmental phenomena and extends throughout the life-span than the child psychology does.

2. Child psychology studies the behaviour of pre-school and school-age children. It only covers the periods from birth to 12 years. On the other hand, developmental psychology covers the entire life-span starting from conception to death.

3. While studying the behaviour of children, child psychology puts more emphasis on the aspects and products of development. On the contrary, developmental psychology puts more emphasis of the process of development. For example, in studying the emotional development, child psychology describes the emotions of the children and what emotional expressions they manifest, while developmental psychology besides describing the emotions and their expressions, concentrates more on explaining the processes of how emotional development takes place, what are the factors associated with it, how emotion changes over time, how emotions affects other dimensions of personality and also suggests ways for attaining emotional stability and maturity.

4. Child psychology gives more importance on the impact of heredity on development. The crucial environmental factors of development find less importance in the study of child psychology; rather emphasis is on discovering the inherited genetic traits and abilities. On the other hand, developmental psychology in its study gives more emphasis on the influence of environment that affects a person's development, besides analysing hereditary influences.

5. Child psychology is unable to predict the development, whereas developmental psychology helps in predicting and sometimes modifying the future development.

6. Child psychology fails to comprehend the continuous nature of development and believes that change occurs in distinct steps and stages. On the other hand, developmental

psychology believes that development is a gradual process.

7. Child psychology assumes that behaviour and developmental aspects are qualitatively different at different stages, while developmental psychology assumes that achievements in behavioural and developmental aspects at one stage is built on previous stages and influence the later stages as well.

SCOPE OF DEVELOPMENTAL PSYCHOLOGY

The scope of modern developmental psychology is so broad that it encompasses everything relating to the development of a person throughout his/her life-span. It studies the products, aspects as well as process of development in all the dimensions of personality starting from conception to old age with an aim to understand, explain, predict, and find out ways and means to ensure development in desirable directions. Researchers are constantly engaged in investigating different aspects of development that opened new vistas in the field and as such the scope of developmental psychology is on gradual enlargement. However, an attempt is made to discuss the subject matter of developmental psychology in the following four broad heads.

1. Stages of Growth and Development

Development starts just after the conception as a result of fertilization of the ovum cell of the mother by the sperm cell of the father. It is only after 280 days stay (approx.)in the mother's womb, the baby gets birth which is the starting of chronological age. The period spent inside the mother's womb is known as prenatal stage and is sub-divided in to three stages viz. stage of conception, embryonic stage and matured embryonic stage. After birth, the postnatal stage starts and it is again generally divided into several stages like infancy, childhood, adolescence, adulthood, and old age. The early developmentalists focused more on infancy and adolescence period because these were considered most significant and crucial stages of development. However, today the story is different. Now the modern developmentalists believe that entire life-span is important. Since development is a continuous process, there is a cause-and-effect relationship among various stages of life so far development is concerned. As such, the subject matter of developmental psychology includes the study of each of the stages of development starting from conception to old age.

2. Domains of Growth and Development

When we talk about the domains of development, it implies the areas or dimensions of personality in which changes occur over time. Development takes place in three fundamental areas-physical, cognitive, and emotional-social. In short, human beings develop when changes occur in their body, mind, spirit, intellect, language, and social relationships. Developmental psychology as a positive branch of psychology incorporates all these domains of behaviour within its vicinity.

Some developmentalists focus on physical development, examining the changes that occur in a person's body, including changes in weight and height; structure and as well process of changes that occur in heart, brain, nervous system, muscles, bones, and other organs etc. and their impact on behaviour pattern.

Cognitive development involves growth and changes occur in intellectual abilities, including changes in sensation, perception, memory, thought, reasoning, language, problem solving skills etc. Developmental psychologists specialised in cognitive domain examines how changes occur in these areas and how these intellectual abilities influence a person's behaviour. They are also keen to investigate how desirable or undesirable changes in the cognitive areas in early stages of life affect development in later stages.

Some other developmentalists are interested in studying the emotional-social domains. Emotional-social development includes changes in a person's personality, emotion, and relationships. Developmentalists in this domain examine stability and changes in the emotional and personality characteristics that differentiate one person from another throughout the life-span. They also investigate how individuals interact with others and their social relationships grow, change, and remain stable over the course of life. Thus, developmental psychology encompasses all the areas of psycho-physical development. It includes all the dimensions of individual's personality-cognitive, affective, and conative in its subject matter of study.

3. Products and Process of Development

While studying changes and stability in various dimensions over the course of life, developmental psychology does not limit itself in describing some specific areas of behaviour, such as speech, emotions or play interests and activities; rather goes deeper and now the interest has been shifted to explain the process of development. For example, in studying the emotional development, developmental psychology not only describes the emotions of people and what emotional expressions they manifest in what situations, rather concentrates more on explaining the processes of how emotional development takes place, what are the factors associated with it, how emotion changes over time, how emotions affect other dimensions of personality as well and suggest ways for attaining emotional stability and maturity. The modern developmental psychologists, besides describing the products of growth, maturation, and learning, focus on how these processes viz. growth, maturation and learning takes place in human life and how they influence the behaviour pattern. Thus, developmental psychology is not only concerned with 'what' of development but also with 'how' of development.

4. Factors and Contexts of Growth and Development

All types of growth and development in human life is broadly the result of two factors namely heredity and environment. The hereditary factors constitute the potentials that an offspring carries from his parents in the form of genes and chromosomes at the time of conception that exerts tremendous influence in the later developments. Hence, it becomes the responsibility of developmentalists to find out how the biological inheritance from parents affects behaviour of the offspring. As such some developmentalists, more particularly the early developmentalists, focused on explaining how genetic background not only determine somatic structure but also how people behave and react to others.

After the heredity, the environment starts to exert its influence in the process of development. The environment in the context of development, according to Urie Bronfenbrenner is of five types- Microsystem, Mesosystem, Exosystem, Macrosystem and chronosystem. The environment, in its totality, in which a person lives, puts significant influence in his/her behaviour patterns; in the rate, nature and direction of development. Hence, to understand the process of development, it is imperative to study the environment in which it occurs. In his ecological approach to development, Urie Bronfenbrenner (1917-2005) (1979, 1986,1997) asserts that the study of development must include the person's interaction with the environment, the person's changing physical and social settings, the relationship among those settings, and how the entire process is affected by the society in which the settings are embedded. Thus, some modern developmentalists investigate the extent to which a person is shaped by his/her early environment and how the current environment influence behaviour in both subtle and evident ways. In this way, the subject matter of modern developmental psychology includes the study of the joint effects of the interaction of heredity and environment in underlining human behaviour.

GOALS OF DEVELOPMENTAL PSYCHOLOGY

The foregoing discussions made under the section- scope of developmental psychology made it clear that the jurisdiction of the subject is multi-dimensional. If some developmentalists are interested in cognitive domain, some others are interested in physical domain, while some others are concentrated on emotional-social developments. Although their interest varies, all the developmental psychologists share one common goal i.e., to understand the growth and change that occur during the course of life. Elizabeth B. Hurlock in her book states six major goals of developmental psychology. These are- (a) to find out what are the characteristic age changes in appearance, behaviour, interests, and goals from one developmental period to another, (b) to find out when these changes occur, (c) to find out under what conditions these changes occur, (d) to find out how these changes influence the child's behaviour, (e) to find out whether, these changes can be predicted, and (f) to find out whether these changes are individual or characteristic of all children.

Developmental psychology aims at optimization of functioning in the early years and compensating the losses with advancing years by helping in detailed understanding of the products and process of development and their determining factors. Within the context of developmental theory across life-span, developmentalists focuses on four major goals viz. describing, explaining, predicting, and finding out ways to control or manage developmental changes. These four major goals are described below.

1. To describe the developmental changes that occur across the life-span

The first and foremost goal of developmental psychology is to describe the developmental milestones. The process of development persists throughout every part of people's lives beginning with the moment of conception and continuing until death. However, at some points of time people continue to grow and change in some domains, while in some other domains their behaviour remains stable. Developmentalists try to describe what changes occur with respect to behaviour characteristic while remaining same in some aspects and at what time they occur. Here, developmental psychology aims to answer 'what' and 'when' of change.

2. To explain the determinants of developmental changes

After describing the aspects of developmental changes, the discipline aims to explain the underlying factors of such changes. It aims to explain how heredity and environmental factors like family, school, peers, religious affiliation etc. influence the changes and developments over time and create individual differences among people. Here, developmental psychology aims to answer 'how' of change.

3. To predict developmental changes

Prediction of changes is the third major goal of developmental psychology. Developmentalists do not limit their effort in describing and explaining the changes, rather aims to predict the future consequences based on the present observations. It tries to forecast the milestones of changes as well as ranges within which changes are likely to occur at a particular stage in one or more aspects or dimensions of personality. For example, with the knowledge of structure of bones during infancy, the developmentalists try to predict the somatic structure and size during adulthood. Here, the developmental psychology aims to answer 'what would be' of change.

4. To find out ways to control or manage developmental changes

Finally, developmental psychology aims to find out the ways and means to bring out desirable changes in various dimensions of personality. Since development is determined by both heredity and environment which are unique to every individual, there is possibility of negative changes in one or more dimensions. Here, the developmental psychology aims to find out useful measures so that interventions can be taken to control and manage them and negative changes can be prevented and compensated.

2

Major Theories and Issues of Developmental Psychology

INTRODUCTION

A theory is a set of interrelated ideas and principles that helps to explain some facts or phenomena. It is 'a way of binding together a multitude of facts so that one may comprehend them all at once'. Theories allow us to understand, explain and predict the world phenomena logically and intelligently and act in a rational way. Thus, theory in developmental psychology implies some set of ideas and information based on scientific evidences to describe, explain, and predict human behaviour and development. They help to explain how individual changes as they age, what are the factors associated with these changes, how and why people behave in a particular manner in a particular situation etc.

Since human development is a complex process occurring in diverse dimensions viz. physical, cognitive, and socio-emotional, and is influenced by so many genetic and environmental factors, no single theory can explain entirely the rich complexity of development. As such, several theories evolved since time immemorial to study changes and stability in different aspects of development in terms of different contexts. If some theories emphasised the process of physical development, some are based on describing and explaining cognitive and socio-emotional development. If some theories try to decode the genetic and biological impact on development, some others give account of the environmental influences on development. However, all the theories, in combination, have contributed to our understanding of human development.

The major theories in developmental psychology can be categorised in the following ways based on their area of concentration.

1. Psychoanalytic Theories
2. Cognitive Theories
3. Behavioural Theories
4. Ethological Theory
5. Ecological Theory
6. Humanistic Theories

PSYCHOANALYTIC THEORIES

The psychoanalytic theories believe that peoples' behaviour is only a surface characteristic and it is controlled and determined by inner forces, feelings, and desires, of which people are unaware. These latent inner forces continually influence behaviour throughout the life-span. Therefore, in order to have a true understanding of developmental characteristics, a careful examination of inner forces, feelings and working of mind is necessary. There are two major psychoanalytic theories.

Sigmund Freud's Psychoanalytic Theory

Sigmund Freud (1856-1939) has contributed his popular psychoanalytic theory in developmental psychology. The assumption of this theory is that human behaviour is the outcome of the impact of unconscious mind, and hence, an understanding of this state of mind can help in comprehending the root causes of behavioural changes. Freud argued that the wishes, desires, and feelings of individuals, more particularly the desires related to sex and agitation, which cannot be fulfilled because of societal prohibitions, are repressed in unconscious mind. Yet, all such repressed and forbidden desires and feelings do not lie permanently in the unconscious mind, rather strives to come up to the level of subconscious and conscious mind, sometimes in disguised forms, in slips of tongue (Freudian slips) and in dreams. Most of our maladaptive and antisocial behaviours are caused by these striving of repressed desires to come up to conscious and subconscious mind. Thus, Freud's psychoanalytic theory believes that the surface of behaviour and personality structure is firmly established by the inner forces and early experiences gained during the child's first five to six years.

According to Freud, the personality involves three aspects- *Id*, *Ego* and *Super ego*. *Id* represents the raw basic staff of the individual and follows the 'pleasure seeking' principle. It instigates the individuals to fulfil their desires in any way without any care for social rules and regulations, and hence makes individuals selfish and unethical. The *ego* develops out of Id and follows the principle of 'reality' and serves as a controlling factor between primitive drives and reality so that the *Id* cannot act irrespective of societal restrictions and hereby helps in integrating the person into the society. *Super ego*, on the contrary, represents a person's conscience and follows the principles of 'perfection'. It is idealistic in nature and helps people to judge right and wrong. It is developed around the age five or six. Thus, Freud emphasised biological and natural forces as determinants of behaviour pattern of people.

Besides the concept of *Id*, *Ego* and *Super ego*, Freud argued that human beings go through five stages of psychosexual development. These are Oral stage- birth to one and half years, Anal stage- one and half to 3 years, Phallic stage- 3 to 6 years, Latency stage- 6 to Puberty and Genital stage-Puberty onwards. During Oral stage, infant's pleasure, and sexual impulses centres on mouth, which is shifted to anus at Anal stage and to genitals at Phallic stage. At the stage of Latency, the child represses sexual impulses and develop social and intellectual skills, while at Genital stage there is reawakening of sexual interests and the source of sexual pleasure shifted to some people outside the family. Thus, according to Freud the 'Sex', which he called 'libido' is the centre of all behavioural manifestation and as such gratification of sexual needs is necessary for balanced development of personality. If sexual needs are not gratified at each stage, the person is bound to lose balance, suffers from frustration, and may lead to the destruction of own life or others, which Freud called 'death instinct'.

However, Freud's psychoanalytic theory has been criticised by many psychologists on several grounds. Firstly, Freud gives importance to a person's natural and biological phenomena; whereas the environmental context of development is completely ignored. Secondly, there is too much emphasis on the role of 'sex' in human life. Freud tried to over generalise all behaviour with sexual impulses. Moreover, Freud's notion that early experiences determine adult behaviour is ruled out by subsequent researchers.

Erik Erikson's Psychosocial Theory

Inspired by the psychoanalytic theory of Freud, an important theory was developed by Erik Erikson, popularly known as psychosocial theory. However, this theory is different form Freudian theory in many aspects. The Freud's theory emphasised the psychosexual development, whereas Erikson's primary concern is psychosocial development, or development within a social context. This theory advocates that our behaviour and personality is shaped by social interaction with other people and cultural influences, unlike Freudian theory that associates our behaviour with sex or 'libido'.

Erickson had suggested eight stages of development, namely the stages of Trust vs distrust-birth to 1 year, Autonomy vs shame and doubt- 2 to 3 years, Initiative vs guild-4 to 5 years, Industry vs inferiority- 6 to puberty, Identity vs identity confusion-adolescence, Intimacy vs isolation-early adulthood, Generativity vs stagnation-middle adulthood and Integrity vs despair-late adulthood. In each stage, according to Erikson, the individual faces some conflicts or crisis that they must strive to resolve. These crisis and conflicts are though not catastrophic, involves both increased vulnerability and enhanced potential. The more efficiently an individual resolve these crises, the healthier the development is. In attempts to resolve these crises, individuals constantly interact with other beings and cultures of society. Thus, Erikson's theory attributes human development as a result of socio-cultural influences, unlike Freudian theory that ascribed development to natural or biological influences.

Erikson's psychosocial theory ruled out Freud's notion that personality is primarily established during first five to six years of life, rather argued that personality continues to develop over the entire life-span and even characterised by improved and flowering of human potential as they grow older. However, psychosocial theory has been criticised on the ground that it gives more emphasis on an image of people that is too much negative.

COGNITIVE THEORIES

Cognition is a mental process involving knowing, learning, and understanding things. It encompasses such phenomena as sensation, perception, imagination, retention, recall, problem solving, reasoning, critical thinking etc. Thus, cognitive theories emphasise on conscious thoughts, unlike psychoanalytic theories which give stress on unconsciousness. These theories attempt to understand how cognitive abilities change as people grow and how individuals' thinking and understanding affects their behaviour. There are three main cognitive theories in developmental psychology.

Piaget's Cognitive Development Theory

Jean Piaget, the famous Swiss psychologist, has unparallel dominance in the field of cognitive development. His central concern was to understand how changes occur in child's mode of thought. Before the emergence of Piaget's theory, the children thought process were assumed as miniature form of adult thought process. Piaget challenged this notion and argued that the thought process of infants and children are both quantitatively and qualitatively distinct to that of adults. Eventually, he described the nature and process of structural as well as functional changes that occur with respect to cognitive domain.

According to Piaget, human beings inherit by birth certain cognitive abilities in order to carry out instinctive and reflex activities like sucking, looking, grasping. Piaget called such cognitive abilities as *'Schemas'*. Thus, one can think of sucking schema, looking schema, or grasping schema. However, these *schemas* or *thought structure*, according to Piaget, changes as children grow because of new experiences and eventually they construct new set of *schemas* or *thought structure*.

Piaget argued that children always engage in continual interaction with different environmental stimuli in order to make *adaptation*. In attempts to make *adaptation*, initially, children try to perceive environmental stimuli in terms of their existing *schemas* or *thought structure*, which Piaget called as process of assimilation. However, at times, when children encounter new stimuli which simply do not fit their existing *schemas* or *thought structure*, they try to incorporate the new experiences to the *existing schemas* or *thought structure* to make it more adequate and relevant. This modified set of *schemas* or *thought structure* again influences childrens new perceptions which are then incorporated to construct more complex *schemas* or *thought structure*. Thus, children keep constructing new *schemas* or *thought structure* in response to encounter with new stimulus, which Piaget called as process of accommodation. In this way, according to Piaget, people organise new knowledge and forms complex thought structure as a result of constant interaction between their biological forces and environmental factors.

Piaget forwarded four stages of cognitive development that extend from infancy to adulthood. The stages are sequential as per age and characterised by distinct ways of understanding the world. Though the stages are age-specific, the ages associated with each stage are only averages and may vary from child to child and culture to culture. These stages are briefly given below.

a. The Sensory-motor Stage

This is the first stage of Piagetian cognitive development. It covers the period from birth to about 2 years of age. In this period infants perceive the world by coordinating their sensory experiences like seeing, hearing, smelling with their physical and motor activities. They directly interact with the environment through sensory and motor activities, for example, sucking, looking, grasping etc.

b. The Pre-operational Stage

The second stage of Piagetian cognitive development is called preoperational stage and covers the period from about 2 to 7 years. At this stage the child goes beyond sensory and motor activity and starts representing world with words, symbols, and images of things. For example, now the child may utter word to ask for something instead of directly reaching out to get it. However, during this stage the child can focus on only one salient feature of a problem at a time and is dominated by immediate appearance of things. This stage is sub-divided in to two stages namely pre-conceptual stage (2 to 4 years) and Intuitive stage (4 to seven years).

c. The Concrete Operational Stage

The third stage of Piagetian cognitive development that lasts from about 7 to 11 years, is called the concrete operational stage. At this stage the child can perform operations and activities that involve concrete objects or examples. They begin to use logical rules to solve problems and can focus on more than one salient feature of a problem and are no longer dominated by physical appearance of things. However, they are not yet ready to perform operations involving abstract ideas and problems.

d. Formal Operational Stage

The fourth and final stage of cognitive development, according to Piaget, is the formal operational stage that appears between 11 and 15 years of age and continues through adulthood. In this stage, the cognitive structure takes a very sophisticated shape and the adolescent can deal with abstract ideas and problems with logical thinking and can engage in scientific thoughts.

Despite providing significant contribution to the field of cognitive development, Piaget's theory has been criticised for several reasons. Firstly, Piaget had described some distinct sets of cognitive skills that appear at a particular chronological age. However, the subsequent developmentalists suggested that certain cognitive skills appear before the age prescribed by Piaget. Secondly, the classification of different stages of cognitive development as per chronological age as given by Piaget may be suitable for western countries but not universally acceptable. Finally, Piaget viewed cognitive development as a discontinuous process, since he classified it into four distinct stages and advocated that the quality of changes in cognitive structure of each stage is different. This notion is criticised by developmentalists on the ground that cognitive development is not necessarily a discontinuous, but a continuous process.

Vygotsky's Socio-cultural Cognitive Theory

Lev Vygotsky (1896- 1934), a Russian developmentalist, is popularly known for his famous socio-cultural theory on cognitive development. This theory provides the theoretical base on how cognitive functions like thinking, reasoning, remembering etc. develop as people grow. Though Vygotsky worked on cognitive development of children like Piaget, he gave far more importance on the influence of social and cultural factors on cognitive development than Piaget did. He argued that human beings constantly construct knowledge by participating in social activities. The development of child's cognition is not possible, according to Vygotsky, by keeping the child away from socio-cultural settings. It is assumed that child's cognitive development occurs as a result of constant interaction of the child with other person in society, by assimilating with different cultural traits of the society, and by learning to use the inventions of society like language, mathematical system etc. The theory advocates that the children learn by observing something happening in the society which they then internalise within themselves. For, example, a child is asked by parents to say 'thank you' to a person for favouring him/her. Then the child might see other people in society saying 'thank you' for favouring them and finally he/she learns to say 'thank you' wherever required, after internalising the meaning of the word and its value in society. Thus, Vygotsky's theory advocates that cognitive development is purely a socio-cultural process and interaction of the child with skilled adult and peers plays a significant role in it.

Bandura's Social Cognitive Theory

American psychologist Albert Bandura is pioneering in social-cognitive theory. This theory is based on the presumption that cognitive development of individual is closely influenced by social environment and behaviour of other people in society. This theory is also known as *observational learning, social learning,* and *social modelling*, as it advocates that learning occurs as a result of observing what and how others do in society. For example, a child who sees his parents quarrelling all the time in small issues, might in turn, quarrel with his/her peers in small issues, showing the same characteristics of his/her parents' behaviour. Thus, according to this theory, people cognitively represent behaviour of others before they adopt such behaviour themselves. In this way, social cognitive theorists stress that people acquire a wide range of behaviours, thoughts, and feelings by imitating others. However, this theory is criticised on the ground that it entirely ignores the developmental changes that can impact our behaviour.

BEHAVIOURAL THEORIES

Behavioural theories, as the name suggests, are concerned with how people learn to behave, and as such these theories take the form of learning theories. Unlike psychoanalytic theories which believe that behaviour is the consequence of inner-feelings and desires of unconscious, the behavioural approach believes that behaviour is the result of continuous exposure of individuals to specific factors of environment. It suggests that observable behaviour and outside stimulus are keys to understand development and hence, for predicting development, critical examination of observable behaviour and their determining environmental factors is necessary. Thus, behavioural theory views that 'nurture' is more important to development than 'nature'. In this regard the statement made by J. B. Watson, the father of behaviourism is worth mentioning. He stated that '*Give me a dozen healthy infants, well-informed, and my own specified world to bring them up in and I'll guarantee to take any one at random and train him to become any type of specialist I might select- doctor, lawyer, merchant-chief, and yes, even beggar-man and thief, regardless of his talents, penchants, tendencies, abilities.*' This statement reflects the extent to which the behavioural theorists believe development is the result of environment.

Behavioural theories also believe that development is completely personal to an individual, and is based on how he/she behaves to environmental stimulus and as such rejects the view that development passes a series of stages. Contrary to Jean Piaget, behaviourists advocate that development is purely quantitative. For example, if a child improves his capacity of logical reasoning as he/she ages, it is not the consequence of changes in the kind of thinking, rather an outcome of achieving greater mental capacities. Historically, behavioural theories emphasised two types of learning namely Classical conditioning and Operant conditioning, which are described below in brief.

Theory of Classical Conditioning

The two pioneers who formulated the theory of classical conditioning in learning are Ivan Pavlov and J.B. Watson. This theory advocated that any desired behaviour can be produced by controlling stimulus in the environment, which in its natural condition does not evoke any response or behaviour. For example, Pavlov in his famous experiment on Dog showed how the dog learns to respond (Secretion of Saliva) to the sound of the bell, to which typically the dog gives no response. The response of the dog was the result of conditioning that occurred as a result of controlling the stimuli, i.e., repeated exposure to the pairing of the sound of the bell and the presentation of the meat. The same technique was applied by Watson in explaining the process of producing and eliminating emotional responses and behaviour with his experiments on human babies. Thus, classical conditioning emphasised that learning or developmental changes are the result of conditioning of observable behaviour through a process of association and substitution of stimulus in the environment.

Theory of Operant Conditioning

The theory of operant conditioning of learning, championed by B.F. Skinner, adopted the similar approach of conditioning of responses as adopted by classical conditioning. But there is a basic difference between the two. In classical conditioning the presence of stimuli is necessary for evoking response. If there is no stimulus no response can be evoked. However, operant condition believes that the presence of known stimuli is not always necessary for evoking response; rather sometimes response can be emitted by unknown stimuli. The individuals deliberately or voluntarily initiate response to unknown stimuli in the environment. They behave in some manner or *operate* in the environment in some way to bring about desired consequences. The environment then reacts to such deliberate responses in the form of reinforcement stimulus, either positive or negative, resulting in repetition or avoidance of the response. If a response follows positive reinforcement, it is repeated in future, while in case the response follows negative reinforcement, it is avoided. Thus, operant conditioning believes that learning or developmental change occurs as a result of strengthening or weakening of a voluntary response by its association of positive and negative consequences.

ETHOLOGICAL THEORY

The ethological theory is based on the presumption that development is influenced by biology. Human beings inherit certain behavioural traits like smiling, crying, just as they carry physical traits. The psychologists who brought ethological theory in prominence include Konrad Lorenz and John Bowlby.

Konrad Lorenz, in his experiments on birds (goose) seen that at a very early stage they develop a strong connection or attachment with their first encounter, may it be their mother or human being or any object. The birds established such attachment, according to Lorenz, in their attempt to survive, and ensure safety and security. Lorenz called such strong attachment of birds with their first encounter as *imprinting*, that can only take place during very early stage, and not possible in later stages. This specific period of early life when *imprinting* takes place is termed as *critical stage* by Lorenz. Since, *imprinting* takes place at very early stage, these are highly resistant to change, irreversible and therefore appears like innate and has long lasting effect in later life.

Some developmental psychologists applied the notion developed by Lorenz based on his experiments on birds into human beings. The most prominent among them is John Bowlby. He analysed the strong attachment, which Lorenz called *imprinting*, developed between human babies and their caretakers during baby's first year of life and concluded that such imprinting or strong bond has important consequences throughout life span. Bowly further argued that if the attachment is positive and secure the individual will develop positively in later stages and if the attachment is negative and insecure, the life-span development will be negative. However, according to Bowlby, though imprinting occurs at a very early stage, which Lorenz called *critical period*, human being develops some attachments at certain time of infancy too, which Bowlby terms as 'sensitive period', in order to promote optimal development of social relationships.

In this way, ethologists conclude that the nature of experiences during early stages of life determines the later behaviour and developmental pattern. However, ethological theory is being criticised on the grounds that it gave too much importance on biological foundations in development and the two stages suggested by the theory as 'critical period' and 'sensitive period' are very rigid.

ECOLOGICAL THEORY

Contrary to ethological theory that explores biological influence on development, ecological theory examines the environmental influences. This theory asserts that development is the outcome of person's constant interaction with the ever changing physical and social environments to which they immersed. Therefore, according to this approach, to understand human development, the environmental context in which it occurs must be explored. Urie Bronfenbrenner (1917-2005) have developed a famous ecological theory which has significant implications in understanding life-span development. Bronfenbrenner asserted that the human development is the reflection of the constant influence of different types of environmental systems. He identified five environmental systems namely micro-system, meso-system, exo-system, macro-system and chrono-system.

Micro-system consists of the network of physical and social settings in which a person lives. For example, siblings, parents, peers, schools, neighbours etc. The influence of this system on behaviour is obvious since it is the settings where individual undergoes most direct interactions each day. The *meso-system* includes the interrelationship between various micro-systems which have profound impact on behaviour pattern. For example, if a child has poor relationship with parents (home setting) might develop issues in developing good relations with teachers (school setting). The environment that is external to individuals, in which they do not have active role to play but influences their behaviour directly or indirectly, consists of *exo-system*. Examples of such settings involve world of work, mass media, government agencies etc. The developing individual may not play any active role in all these social settings but influenced by them. For example, a husband facing difficulty in workplace may carry his tension to home and behave rudely with his wife. The *macro-syste*m is the cultural pattern in which individuals live. The behaviour patterns, beliefs, values etc. of the group in which peoples live has constant impact of behaviour pattern. Finally, Urie Bronfenbrenner had talked about *chrono-system* to examine the impact of time factor on all other systems.

Chrono-system refers that not only the individual changes with time but the society changes as well, which in turn influences the way individuals behave. For example, if a father dies when his child is 7 years old, it will have a different impact on the child's behaviour than if the father dies when he/she is 25 years old.

Thus, ecological theory as the term implies, primarily based on examining a wide range of environmental influences on development. Though Bronfenbrenner in subsequent years had tried to add the biological factors, the theory is often criticised for giving very little importance on that.

HUMANISTIC THEORY

In 20th century a new approach had evolved in studying human development that sees human beings as something different from other creatures who are capable of not only accepting themselves, others, and environment in which they live, but also capable to intervene the environment in order to achieve freedom, self-fulfilment, and strong identities. Therefore, the objective of developmental studies should be to maximize human potentials for self-direction and freedom of choice, building self-esteem and achieve self-actualisation. Because of the extended emphasis it puts on increasing human potentials, the theory representing this perspective is called humanistic theory.

Abraham Maslow and *Carl Rogers* are among the prominent humanistic psychologists, who argued that human beings have some needs that must be fulfilled in order to fulfil the other developmental needs. In fact, Maslow had suggested a concept known as *hierarchy of needs* where he identified three kinds of needs that must be satisfied in a hierarchical order in order to attain maximum development. These *are Fundamental needs,Psychological needs and Self-Actualisation needs*. In the bottom, Maslow placed the fundamental physiological needs like hunger, thirst, and sex. Above the fundamental physiological needs, there are psychological needs like needs of love, affection, self-esteem etc. At the top are those needs which are required for realising one's unique potential to its fullest which Maslow called self-actualisation needs. The fundamental needs of people must be fulfilled before an individual is free to progress to psychological needs, which must be satisfied in order to realise self-actualisation needs. Once the person achieves self-actualisation, they become autonomous and independent. Self-actualised peoples are democratic, problem-centred and can control their destinies and shape the world around them.

Thus, humanistic theory aims not only to increase scientific body of knowledge regarding the pattern and process of development, rather its primary concern is the improvement of human conditions to attain self-actualisation i.e., development of potentials at their fullest. However, the theory is criticised on the ground that it investigates behaviour by relying on intuition and insight.

ISSUES OF DEVELOPMENTAL PSYCHOLOGY

Understanding of the different theories as discussed above, makes it clear that the developmental psychologists have been encountered with some issues relating to the nature and factors of human development. Some theories viewed development as the result of heredity factors, while some other put more emphasis on environmental influences. There are theories that described development in distinct stages, while others viewed development as a gradual and cumulative process. Moreover, some developmentalists argued that early experiences are very rigid and as such persist throughout the life-span, while others advocated that early experiences change over time. In this way, the different theories gave birth of three important issues in human development, namely (a) Nature vs Nurture issue, (b) Continuity vs Discontinuity issue and (c) Stability vs Change issue.

1. Nature Vs Nurture Issue

The nature vs nurture issue is aroused out of the examination of hereditary and environmental influences on development. Nature refers to the biological inheritance, while nurture refers to the environment. Thus, nature-nurture issue involves the extent to which an individual is the product of heredity and environment. The naturists argue that development is influenced by the potentials that the child inherits by birth. Though they acknowledge that extreme hostile environmental factors can depress development in a superficial manner, but it has nothing to do with the basic growth tendencies. The ecological theory of John Bowlby and Freudian theory of psychoanalysis etc. are examples that give stress on the hereditary influence on development.

On the contrary, the proponents of the importance of nurture advocate that heredity is insignificant in development, rather it is the result of constant environmental influences. The supporters of environment claims that environmental influences are the determining factors of development. The behavioural theories of Watson, Pavlov, and Skinner; Socio-cultural cognitive theory of Vygotsky and Bandura, ecological theory of Urie Bronfenbrenner, psychosocial theory of Erikson etc. are examples of developmental theories that are based on environmental perspective.

There has been an assumption for long that an individual is mostly the product of genetic influences and environmental alterations and life style choices are not heritable. But recent research investigations found that individual's life experiences can be passed down to children or next generations. As such, the impact of environmental forces in development got attention in subsequent times.

To assess the environmental foundations of development, research studies were conducted on both animals and human beings. Among studies conducted on animals, some healthy male rats having no pre-existing genetic disposition to become diabetic were fed high-fat-diet that may develop symptoms of Type 2 diabetes and found that the daughters of the investigated rats developed symptoms of Type 2 diabetes even after eating normal food. (Skinner, 2010). Among individuals, tremendous studies have been undertaken on twins- both monozygotic and dizygotic, adopted children, siblings of shared environmental experiences as well as non-shared environmental experiences and concluded environment as a significant factor in development. A research study found that a monozygotic twin has close to 50 percent risk of developing schizophrenia when other twin develops the disorder (Hanson & Gottesman, 2005). Here, if the genetic factors were the sole cause, the risk of a monozygotic twin to become schizophrenic would have been 100 percent when the other twin develop the disorder.

Thus, it is evident that not only genetic factors but also the environment to which an individual is exposed, plays a significant role towards growth and development. In fact, environment plays its role not only after birth, rather just after conception. The environment in the mother's womb (internal environment) during pregnancy like mother's physical and mental health, nutrition taken, uterine crowding, any accident or incidents, toxins, emotional states etc. exerts influences on growth and development of the fetus. The environment present at the time of birth like hygienic or unhygienic environment, stress and anxiety during birth etc. plays significant influences on later developments. After birth, the physical, socio-cultural, and psychological environment starts playing their role in shaping personality and continues till death.

2. Stability Vs Change Issue

The stability vs change issue involves whether the early traits and characteristics change with time or they persist throughout life-span. The supporters of stability notion believe that the early traits, developed as a result of heredity influence and possibly by early experiences, are so rigid, irreversible and as such these stay throughout the life-span. For example, if a child remained shy during his early years, he would remain shy and reserved with others throughout the life-span. Sigmund Freud and John Bowlby can be categorised as supporter of this notion. Freud holds that personality is primarily established during first five to six years of life. Similarly, John Bowlby in his ethological theory asserted the imprinting or the strong attachment established between the baby and caretaker during early stage influences the emotional behaviour throughout life.

On the contrary, developmentalists who advocate the change notion argue that the early traits and characteristics are not stable, rather changes in later stages of life as a result of constant environmental influences. People behave or operate in ever changing environment in order to make adjustments and accordingly changes the early traits which becomes irrelevant at times in the environmental contexts. Jean Piaget supports the change notion in his theory of cognitive development. He argued that in the form of *accommodation* to new stimuli, children construct new set of *schemas* or *thought structure.*

3. Continuity Vs Discontinuity Issue

The issue of continuity and discontinuity involves whether development is a continuous process or it occurs abruptly in distinct stages of life. The supporters of continuity notion hold that development is a gradual and cumulative process that continues throughout life. It is not possible to separate development from one stage to another, rather it follows orderly sequence of change. In speech development, for example, though it seems that during infancy the baby utters words abruptly and in childhood he/she speaks fluently, the development cannot be said as something that occurred distinctly in infancy and childhood period, rather it is the result of continuous practice from infancy to childhood. The developmentalists who emphasise that development is the result of environmental influences, generally describe it as continuous.

On the contrary, some developmentalists, basically those who believe development is the result of hereditary influence, hold that development occurs in distinct manner in different stages. It is not the result of continuous changes, rather each stage is characterised by distinct or unique developmental characteristics. For example, in certain stage the child is unable to deal with abstract phenomena, but in later stages he/she could able to deal abstractions. The theories of Sigmund Freud, Erik Erikson and Jean Piaget follow this notion.

3

Methods of Developmental Psychology

INTRODUCTION

Scientific methods may be described as precise, objective, and verifiable procedures, ways and means to investigate some phenomena, events, attributes, relationships etc., developed and used by experts, and in which the experimenter is not swayed by prejudice or opinion. Regarding the adoption of scientific approach in child development, it is stated earlier that Pestalozzi published the first scientific record of the development of a young child in the year 1774 based on the observational notes of his three and half year-old son. Later, psychologists like Tiedemann of Germany, Millicent Shinn of America had contributed in the study of young children by publishing biographical notes of development of young children based on their own observations. However, studies on children in a more scientific way (based on actual observation of developing children) were started in the second half of the 19th century, when Charles Darwin had published a short paper based on the detailed observation on the development of his own infant son, Doddy, in 1877, for which he is often credited with introducing the first scientific methods to the study of development.

Thus, the emergence of scientific procedures in studying child behaviour can be traced back to later part of 19th century only. Lack of suitable methods of investigation is one of the various reasons of researcher's indifference and disinterest towards the field. In this regard J.B. Watson in the early part of 20th century pointed out that '*......no well-trained men or women has ever watched the complete and daily development of a child from its birth to its third year? Plants and animals we know about because have studied them, but the human child until very recently has been a mystery'*. Eventually, innovative and varied methods and techniques started appearing significantly in 20th century.

Today, developmental psychology in its study of growth, change and stability adopts a robust scientific approach. Like members of other scientific disciplines, researchers in developmental psychology test their hypotheses about the nature and course of development by applying scientific methods. These methods are many and varied. Some methods are relatively uncontrolled; while others are highly controlled with regard to some particular domains as well as samples. Hence, several factors need to be considered while selecting a particular method for investigation. A few among these are (a) nature of the problem or behaviour to be studied, (b) age levels of the subjects to be studied, (c) orientation and resourcefulness of the researcher (d) availability of materials and subjects, (e) other limiting factors such as time and financial resources etc. and (f) ethical obligations. For the purpose of readers, some of the better-known methods are explained as under.

HISTORICAL METHODS

Historical methods are the process in which systematic examination of past events are made. It is not just finding out facts or dates, rather a description of the past events that involves an interpretation attempt to recapture the events or phenomena. These methods employ specific techniques and guidelines by which researchers analyse data and evidences in order to describe the past events, explain their influence on the present events and to forecast possible future occurrences. Developmental psychologists use historical methods to gain an understanding of the various developmental phenomena of the early stages in order to describe the present behaviour characteristics and to predict the nature, rate, and direction of future development. The common methods used by developmentalists that can be categorised under historical methods are described below.

Biographical Method

Biographical method, as the term implies is a method of investigating a phenomenon by analysing the biography of an individual. The biography is compiled and constructed by observing and recording all the particulars in real time, in a diary, pertaining to a particular behaviour or developmental changes as they occur, by intelligent observers. Eventually, the biography is analysed and interpreted to draw conclusions regarding the manifestation of certain behaviour or developmental changes and their underlying causes.

Biographical method is one of the important methods being widely used in developmental studies. In fact, the initial studies undertaken systematically on young children were in the form of *baby biography*. To mention some of the prominent developmentalists who kept records of child's development and their behaviour characteristic are Charles Darwin, Tiedemann, Millicent Shinn, Preyer, and Moore. Charles Darwin had recorded and published a short paper based on the detailed observation on the development of his own infant son, Doddy, in 1877. Millicent Shinn's record on the development of her young niece is a most useful document in developmental psychology.

As mentioned earlier, in biographical method a detailed day to day records of the child's behaviour is maintained. Intelligent observers, usually parents or close relatives who are well acquainted with the child, maintain a diary, and took time and trouble to note down the milestone of development and behavioural characteristics as well as situations evoking different responses throughout different stages of child's growth and development.

Afterwards, the biographers proceed to analyse the biographies. A delightful construct of the biography and its objective analysis gives useful insight into the nature, rate, directions, and milestones of development throughout the developmental stages.

However, the effectiveness of biographical method depends on so many factors. To mention- orientation as well as mental process of the biographer, overcoming difficulties in generalisation etc. are significant. Any individual capable of scientific detachment can compile and analyse a child biography. But, these cannot be regarded reliable since the job requires sound orientation into the laws and theories of psychology. In most cases the biographers are the parents or other close relatives who are not trained enough to note down scientifically the significant particulars. Thus, there is possibility of biased observation, recording as well as interpretation of facts. Even Charles Darwin has been questioned by psychologists and criticised that he failed in keeping distinct records and valid analysis of them. The mental process of the biographer is the second obstacle of child biographies. The biographers being adults often tend to project their adult-like emotions, attitudes, and prejudices on the child's mental working. Finally, inability to generalise the findings revealed through biographical method in a greater context is its third drawback. In biographical method a child or a group of children are investigated in relation to some environmental conditions. The findings, revealed thereby, can represent that child or group of children but not all-other children of the same sex and age, and hence universal laws cannot be derived based on that. Thus, biographical method lacks efficiency in generalisation of its evidences.

Case Study Method/Clinical Method

Case study as a research method involves an up-close, in-depth, and detailed examination of a particular 'case'. The case may be an individual, organisation, event or action in a specific time and place. Case study method is widely used by scientists in a wide range of fields ranging from psychology, sociology, anthropology, political science, education, social work and so on.

In developmental psychology case study is used in understanding a person's mind, behaviour and other developmental attributes based on his/her past experiences. It is a longitudinal design that focuses on a single individual, rather than a group of individuals. Here, the researcher tries to go deep into the past experiences of the individual in order to find out the important factors which are responsible for the present behaviour. The detailed information about the subject's past experiences are collected through interviewing the subject, his/her parents and other close relatives; through screening past medical records; through observing present behaviour and so on. Thus, case study provides a dramatic, in-depth portrayal of an individual's life and can help in accumulating developmental information. A good deal of early work of Jean Piaget, a Swiss developmentalist, was based on case study approach. Piaget's famous theory on cognitive development is the upshot of the hypotheses which he formulated through careful observation of three cases i.e., his three children namely- Lucienne, Laurent, and Jacqueline.

Case study occupies a prominent place in clinical treatment. Mental health professionals mostly employ this technique for the purpose of diagnosing behavioural problems to provide effective interventions. The therapists are of the view that case studies help the patients reconstruct their own past histories, which in turn can resolve their inner conflicts. Because of wider application in clinical purposes, case study method is often known as clinical method.

However, the generalisation of findings from case study is often problematic. Since the data are collected on only one child or individual, who is unique in terms of genetic make-up and personal experiences, hence it is difficult to generalise the findings to a larger population. Secondly, effective case study requires sufficiently trained and expert professionals who can scientifically interpret the past experiences of the subject and draw inferences therefrom. But in practice, it is seen that a researcher rarely ensures that other researchers are agreed with his/her findings.

DESCRIPTIVE METHODS

Descriptive methods are those methods of investigation which attempt to describe and interpret what exists at present in the form of conditions, practices, social units, trends, effects, attitudes, beliefs, behaviours etc. It is concerned with the phenomena that are typical of the normal conditions. Descriptive methods are used in developmental psychology to observe, record, and describe the extent to which people develop with respect to developmental milestones throughout different developmental stages. Though descriptive research cannot prove what causes a behaviour, yet can reveal important information about people's behaviour. For example, what are the emotions of a 6-year-old child and how he/she expresses emotional behaviour can be effectively studied through descriptive methods. However, to what extent a particular emotion is the result of parental love and affection cannot be studied under descriptive methods. The common methods and techniques of data collection under descriptive methods are described below.

Observation

Generally, we observe things around us all the time, but this sort of ordinary observation does not have characteristics of a scientific method, since they are not systematic and organized. Observation becomes a scientific method of study when it is systematically planned and designed to serve specific purposes and proceed in an orderly sequence. In this method the observer observes the behaviour of an individual or group of individuals either in natural or controlled settings and records the observation with the help of notepad, video-tape, audio-tape recorder, or any other devices. Afterwards, the observed behaviour is analysed and interpreted to derive conclusions. Thus, observation uses indirect approach and tries to estimate the mental process of subjects through observing their external behaviour. Though observation is one of the significant methods of developmental psychology, it requires an important set of skills. For observation to be effective, the observer while using this method should have some idea about (a) What to be observed, (b) Who to be observed, (c) When to be observed,

(d) Where to be observed, (e) How to be observed and (f) How the observation to be recorded.

Observation as a method of scientific investigation can be classified in two ways. With regard to the nature of participation of the observer, it is of three types, namely participant observation, non-participant observation and disguised observation. When the observer observes by becoming a member of the group which he/she is observing, it is called participant observation. Conversely, when the observer observes the group as a detached emissary, such observation is called a non-participant observation. Again, in some cases the observer,though participates with the person/group he/she is observing, yet his/her presence is not known to them. This type of observation is called disguised observation. In spite of the pros and cons, almost all types of observations are being used in studying child behaviour. Participant observation is mostly used to investigate cultural questions. In participant observation, sometimes known as ethnography, the researcher lives for a period of weeks, months or even years in another culture in order to understand the culture,values, and attitudes with an aim to estimate how culture, ethnicity, race etc. influence child behaviour and developmental pattern. Secondly, in situations where the observer thinks that his participation may not evoke the natural or actual behaviour of the child, non-participant observation is applied. For example, a child may not manifest his anti-social behaviour when he/she knows that he/she is being observed, rather will try to manipulate the behaviour that is considered socially unacceptable. In such cases the observer does not participate with the child, rather would employ non-participant observation. However, in non-participant observation the observer cannot experience what the members of the group being observed, are experiencing. As such, there is possibility of subjective biasness on the part of the observer in interpreting the child behaviour. Finally, disguised observation is employed where the observer's participation is necessary, but child's knowledge about observer's presence may disturb or affect the event or behaviour. This type of observation, if administered properly, can yield greater accuracy, reliability, and validity of the findings.

Because, in one hand the observer himself/herself experiences what the child (subject) experiences, and hereby minimizes subjective biasness of the observer in interpretation, and on the other hand there is maximum possibility that the child manifests his/her actual behaviour, since he/she is being observed is not known to him/her.

Regarding environmental context, observation can be classified in two types, namely *naturalistic observation* and *controlled* or *laboratory observation*. When observation is made in real-world setting without disturbing or affecting the events or phenomena, it is called naturalistic observation. On the other hand, when observation is conducted in controlled settings, it is called laboratory or controlled observation. In child development naturalistic observation is mostly used, where researchers intensively watch behaviour as it occurs and records it by means of paper-pencil or other electronic gadgets. It is most useful in studying the developmental characteristics of a child's habits, interests or other personality traits. For example, the effects of parental involvement in emotional development of a child can be determined by observing the child in a natural setting of his day-to-day life. Similarly, if a researcher tries to investigate the reasons of anti-social behaviour of a child, he/she will wait till the behaviour occurs and then use all the resources to observe, record and interpret the behaviour under natural conditions. Thus, naturalistic observation provides insights that a researcher sometimes my not achieve through controlled observation. The major advantage of naturalistic observation, to mention- is the independence of the subject's ability as well as willingness to participate in the observation. There are situations when child hesitates to participate with the observer, lacks insight to talk to the observer about certain aspects of the behaviour, tries to hide or alter illegal or deviant behaviour. In all such cases naturalistic observation serves very useful purpose. However, naturalistic observation is not free from limitations. It is not a strong technique to test hypothesis, since the observer does not have any control over any behaviour of the child, the manipulation of the independent variable to test cause-and-effect relationship with the dependent variable is not possible. Moreover, in naturalistic observation, the effects of extraneous variables cannot be controlled. Again, there is possibility of subjective biasness of the observer as he/she may have some expectations, may look for some behaviour and in turn may record as such. Another strong demerit of naturalistic observation is that it has been and can be widely used to observe the young children's behaviour in nursery or preschool settings, but much harder to use in studying adult behaviour.

Since naturalistic observation is not fruitful in testing cause-and-effect relationship, developmental psychology often uses controlled observation in a laboratory setting where many of the complex factors of the real world, which determines the behaviour but not the focus of the investigation, can be controlled. For example, a researcher intends to observe how an 8 year-old child reacts when he/she sees other people act aggressively. Here, if the researcher tries to observe the child in natural setting like home or school, he/she cannot control the manner how other people act aggressively, to what extent the child experience aggression, who do the child sees acting aggressively etc. Conversely, in laboratory setting the researcher, keeping in view the demand of the study can control all these factors. Here, he/she can control on how other people will act aggressively in front of the child, to what extent they will show aggression in front of the child and who will act aggressively. Thus, in laboratory or controlled observation the researchers have more confidence about how to interpret his/her observation. However, the efficiency of this method is often criticized due to several reasons. It is argued that the laboratory setting is unnatural and therefore can cause the child to behave unnaturally. Sometimes the participants (child) may be intimidated by the unfamiliar laboratory setting.

Questionnaire and Opinionnaire

Questionnaire is a structured form, in written format, consisting of a set of questions designed to collect data regarding some phenomena, events, habits, behaviours etc. from one or more respondents. The questions in the questionnaire may be close-ended, open-ended or a combination of both. In close-ended questionnaire, every question accompanies alternative responses from where the respondents are asked to select, tick, or strike out the answer that they fancy or that closely fits them. Whereas in open ended questionnaire, no such alternative answers are given, rather the respondents are allowed free hand and are asked to provide their own answers. Since in open-ended questionnaire, the respondents are allowed to record their own opinion, it is sometimes known as opinionnaire. Thus, questionnaire is a self-reporting method. It can be administered face to face, through postal correspondence and more recently through internet. The questionnaire technique becomes more useful especially when there are many respondents. As it can be effectively used in collecting information from large number of respondents, it is sometimes referred to as survey method.

In developmental studies questionnaire method was first used by G. Stanley Hall of America while investigating the children's perception on quantity and quality in a school in Boston, which included 123 questions. The modern developmental psychologists use questionnaire in bringing out specific information on certain aspects of behaviour and personality. Personality attributes like judgements, feelings, beliefs, values, attitudes, convictions etc. can effectively be addressed with the help of a questionnaire. For example, a researcher intending to find out the value pattern of adolescents, can easily prepare a questionnaire consisting a set of questions representing different values and administer on a group of adolescents. Similarly, a wide range of topics from religious beliefs to drug habits to criminal behaviour to sexual habits to perception on various phenomena etc. can be studied through questionnaires.

However, the effectiveness of a questionnaire is often challenging. There is always a tendency of the respondents to answer in a way that is socially desirable, rather to report what they think or feel. For example, to a question *'what would you do during waiting time in a platform?'*, the respondent may try to exhibit himself/herself in a better light and may select the option *'I would read magazine'*, while actually he/she would love to spend waiting time roaming here and there or watching television. Again, if the questions use tough language or in case of vague questions, the respondents may not give answer or give wrong answer because he/

she does not understand the question. Similarly, if the questionnaire includes many questions, the respondent either may become reluctant to answer or may answer randomly in a monotonous way without even trying to understand, and thereby increases the possibility of mistakes in interpretation. However, taking special care in constructing questionnaire, the developmentalists have been using questionnaires in exploring various attributes more particularly the personality traits.

Interview

Interview is a face to face, sometimes technology mediated, method of eliciting information by researchers from the respondents regarding some facts, beliefs, values, feelings etc. Like questionnaire, here the researcher (interviewer), a skilled person, asks the respondents (interviewee) a set of questions which the interviewee is supposed to answer. However, it is different from the questionnaire in three respects. First, in interview the questions are asked orally, though pre-determined and written on a piece of paper; where as in questionnaire, the questions are asked in written form. Second, in interview the responses are recorded by the interviewer with the help of paper-pencil or some electronic gadgets like audio-recorder, video-recorder, CCTV etc., while in questionnaire the respondents themselves record their responses in written form. Third, like questionnaire, interview cannot be carried out to large number of respondents at a time. It is a man-to-man endeavour.

There are two types of interviews- structured and unstructured. In structured interview, the questions to be asked are pre-planned and pre-determined as per the objectives of the study. Here, the interviewer does not ask additional questions which are not pre-determined. Conversely, in unstructured interview, though the 'to be asked questions' are pre-determined, the interviewer can ask further questions if need arises.

Developmental psychologists employ interview for the purpose of understanding different personality traits as well as for treating maladjusted behaviour. Interview method was famously used by

Jean Piaget in studying children. In studying the nature of child cognition, Piaget asked numerous questions about causality and natural phenomena and thus demonstrated that child thinking differed essentially from adult thinking. In Interview method, the child, or the individual presents before the psychologist who after establishing rapport asks a variety of questions, either pre-determined or constructed at the spur of the moment, the responses to which by the child are recorded in real time. However, a skilled psychologist generally uses tape-recorder for recording the responses of the respondents, because if the child notices that his/her responses are being recorded, he/she may become unnatural and give artificial responses. The psychologist, besides asking questions and recording responses, observes the para language of the child i.e., his/her facial expressions, eye contacts, body language and general conduct etc. Thus, in interview method, the psychologists not only get formal information from what the child speaks but also can draw inferences from how the child speaks. Eventually, the information are processed and evaluated with the help of a score card or rating scale to arrive at conclusions.

Though interview is an important technique of developmental study, it is not free form drawbacks. Sometimes the respondents do not like to share their innermost secrets and hesitate to reveal something derogatory to themselves. For example, in an interview an individual may say he/she does not take drugs even though actually he/she does. To overcome this difficulty, establishing a close rapport between the interviewer and the interviewee is crucial. Moreover, lack of skills and experiences on the part of the psychologists often create problems in recording and evaluating the responses. Sometimes, interview is conducted over telephone which lacks credibility, since there is absence of observation of the general conduct by the psychologist.

Psychological Tests

Standardised psychological tests have long been used for a variety of psychological, educational, cultural, and sociological studies of groups as well as of individuals. These are devised and used primarily for the determination of individual differences in two areas viz. general intelligence and personality traits such as aptitude, attitude, perception, feeling, likes and dislikes, thinking, values etc. The common fields in which psychological tests are effectively used in developmental studies are the nature and course of mental development, nature, milestones and factors of emotional and social development, intellectual and non-intellectual personality differences among individuals with respect to various factors like age, sex, racial membership, religion etc.; differences that might be attributed to hereditary or to environmental factors, intellectual and other personality traits of a typical groups such as the mentally gifted, the mentally retarded, the neurotic, and the psychotic etc.

Good psychological tests are highly standardized, follows uniform procedures for administration and scoring. Proper techniques are taken to ensure validity, reliability, and norms while construction of psychological tests to ensure valid and reliable measurement. One such important test is the Stanford-Binet Intelligence test to measure IQ of children of different ages. Now a days, developmentalists have constructed many psychological tests to measure and identify various facts of individuals. In India, one can easily purchase standardized psychological tests to measure different behaviour traits and developmental aspects from the National Psychological Corporation (NPC), located at Agra and other psychological organizations.

The psychological tests are also been used in clinical purposes for diagnosis of different personal problems related to intelligence, behaviour, attitudes, emotions, social relations, and other personality problems. These include different types of intelligent tests, reaction time tests, projective techniques etc. Through projective techniques the totality of personality is estimated. The nature of unconscious mind is studied by revealing repressed feelings and desires. There are different types of projective techniques like Rorschach Ink Blot test, Murray's Thematic Apperception Test (TAT), Travis Johnston Projection test etc.

Psychological tests, though have wider application, are not free from criticism. One such criticism is that while administration, a psychological test does not consider situational context. They consider behaviour as consistent and stable, while in reality, behaviour varies with respect to situations. For example, a person may score poor in an intelligence test in an anxious environment like office setting, but may score much higher in a calm environment like home setting. Secondly, psychological tests, though measures different psychological aspects, the results are not absolute, rather relative. They cannot claim reliability and validity as claimed by physical tests. Finally, 'culture fair' is the most important aspect, for which most psychological tests are being criticised. 'Culture fair' of a psychological test specifies a test which is free from cultural bias so that no one culture has advantage over another. To ensure this, every effort should be made in construction of the test so that no aspect or issues are included in the test which relies on knowledge specific to a particular culture.

CORRELATIONAL METHODS

All the above discussed methods categorized under historical and descriptive methods help in observing, recording, and describing the extent to which an individual changes throughout different stages or ages, but these methods are inefficient to reveal the relationship of a particular behaviour characteristic with other. However, in developmental studies, only description of behaviour characteristics or personality traits in different stages is not sufficient, rather an understanding of the relationship of a particular behaviour characteristic with other aspects is crucial. This helps in comprehending the process of development, predicting development as well as suggesting interventive measures to stimulate future development in desirable directions. For example, the knowledge of the description of milestones of physical development at the age of 5 years of a child may give some important information about the status of physical development of the child, but helps no way in predicting as well as enhancing physical development in later stages, unless and until the correlated factors of physical development are identified. Correlational methods serve such purposes very effectively.

As noted earlier, correlational methods are much advance than historical and descriptive methods and goes beyond describing the behaviour. In this method attempts are made to identify the relationship between two or more variables which in turn helps in predicting future behaviour. In simple words, correlational method examines whether two variables are associated or correlated to each other. Its goal is to describe the strength and direction of relationship between two variables, which is expressed by a mathematical score, called *Coefficients of Correlations* that ranges from -1 to +1. A positive coefficient of correlation implies positive relationship between the two variables indicating that an increase in the magnitude of one variable coincides corresponding increase in the other variable or vice-versa. Similarly, a negative coefficient of correlation implies negative relationship between the two variables indicating that an increase in the magnitude of one variable coincides corresponding decrease in the other variable or vice versa. The higher the value of coefficients of correlation (whether positive or negative), the stronger the relationship between the variables. If the value is 0, it implies that the variables are not related in any way, neither positive nor negative. After knowing the strength and direction of relationship between two variables, it becomes very easy to predict the one with the other. For example, to study whether parental permissiveness is related with their children's self-control, the researcher needs to record the degree of parent's permissiveness as well as their children's self-control. Afterwards, the researcher would analyse the data on parent's permissiveness as well as children's self-control with the help of statistical techniques like 'r test' to find out the coefficients of correlation that might ranges from -1 to +1. Now, with the help of this calculated coefficients of correlation, the researcher could easily draw inference as whether the two variables i.e., parent's permissiveness and children's self-control are related with each other or not; if related, what is the direction of the relationship- positive or negative and how strong the relationship is. Afterwards, it would become very easy to predict the one with the other.

Though a correlational method, as described in forgoing paragraphs, provides important information regarding the strength and direction of relationship between variables, and in turn helps in making prediction; is not effective in studying the cause-and-effect relationship between variables. For instance, the calculated positive relationship between parent's permissiveness and children's self-control may mean that an increase in parental permissiveness coincides corresponding increase in children's self-control and vice-versa, but this neither mean that permissive parenting necessarily causes high self-control in children, nor does it mean that high self-control in children causes their parents to be more permissive. Similarly, the calculated negative relationship between parent's permissiveness and children's self-control may mean that an increase in parental permissiveness coincides corresponding decrease in children's self-control and vice-versa, but this does not mean that permissive parenting necessarily causes low self-control in children. It could mean that, but it could also mean that low self-control in children causes their parents to become more permissive. Since manipulation of variables is not possible in correlational methods, hence, it could also mean that other intervening variables like heredity or poverty caused low self-control in children. Thus, correlational method helps in understanding the strength and direction of relationship between variables, but cannot help in studying causal relationship between variables, that means it cannot say which one is the cause and which one is the effect.

EXPERIMENTAL METHODS

As noted, in correlational method causal relationship between variables cannot be studied as there is no manipulation of variables. In contrast, experimental methods are designed to study the cause-and-effect relationship between two or more variables, since variables are manipulated and participants can be randomly assigned. Watson and Gesell are the best-known psychologists who utilized experimental method in child study.

The experimental method is a carefully regulated procedure where the researcher assigns independent and dependent variables to the experiment and identifies the intervening variables. The independent variables are the experimental variables which are manipulated and influential, and are believed to effect dependent variables. They are called independent because these variables can be manipulated by the researcher independently of other factors to see its effect. On the other hand, dependent variables are those which are believed to be dependent upon the independent variables or which may change as a result of the change or manipulation in the independent variables. The intervening variables are those which exercise their impact upon the dependent variables, but are not the focus of the experiment and hence need to be controlled. The researcher intending to study the causes of a particular behaviour (dependent variable) would manipulate those factors (independent variables) that are believed to influence that behaviour, while making the other intervening variables constant. If the behaviour under study changes when a factor is manipulated, it can be said that the manipulation of the factor has caused the behaviour to change. In other words, the variations in the behaviour (dependent variable) are attributed to the changes in the independent variables. Thus, in experimental method the causal relationship between variables are investigated by manipulating the independent variables to see its effect on dependent variables.

In developmental studies, for instance, a researcher wants to study the causal relationship between exposure to televised aggression and subsequent aggressive behaviour of children. For that purpose, the researcher, first, may formulate a hypothesis that exposure to televised aggression causes aggressive behaviour among children. Here, exposure to televised aggression would be the independent variable and the aggressive behaviour would be dependent variable, since it is hypothesized that aggressive behaviour is dependent upon exposure to televised aggression. The other factors that might exert influence on aggressive behaviour like socio-economic status, parental over protectiveness, violence at home etc. are intervening variables. To test the hypothesis, the researcher would manipulate independent variable (exposure to televised aggression) to see its impact on aggressive behaviour of children by controlling the intervening variables (socio-economic status, parental over protectiveness, violence at home etc.). The researcher may form two groups of children- experimental group and control group. The experimental group is a group whose experience would be manipulated. A control group is the comparison group that is as much like the experimental group but whose experience would not be manipulated. However, utmost care is to be taken in forming the two groups. Random assignment technique is adopted in assigning children in each of the group, which means that the researcher assigns children to experimental and control group by chance. This reduces the impact of intervening variables on the dependent variable by ensuring that the two groups are identical before starting the experiment and there is no pre-fixed condition. Afterwards, the experimental group would be exposed to a good deal of aggression on television in the form of murder, crime shows, shootings, violence and so on, and the control group would not be exposed to such events or may be exposed to television imaginary that does not contain any kinds of aggression. Subsequently, the behaviour of both the groups would be tested with respect to aggression. If the results show that the children in experimental group are more aggressive than the children in control group, it would be concluded that exposure to televised aggression causes aggressive behaviour among children. In this way, experimental method provides most objective and reliable information regarding causal relationship between variables.

However, experimental method suffers from drawbacks. The effectiveness of the method depends upon the ability to control the intervening variables, which is done by random assignment of participants in to experimental group as well as control group. But, the requirement of random assignment, sometimes, may not be possible for ethical or practical reasons. For example, in studying the effect of parental love and affection on children's emotional behaviour, it would be unethical to design an experiment in which a group of children is prevented from getting parent's love and affection. Second, the conduct of experiment in controlled setting may alter the natural behaviour pattern of the participants and thus decreases the ecological validity of the results. Third, in developmental psychology some variables are not easy to manipulate such as age, gender, socio-economic status, abusive family etc.

QUASI EXPERIMENTAL METHODS

The prefix 'quasi' means 'resembling' and thus quasi experiments implies a method of investigation that is not but resembles experimental method. In other words, quasi experiment is a method which is designed much like experimental method except the random assignment of participants in experimental and control group. The main component of true experimental method is random assignment of the participants into experimental and control group, meaning every participant has the equal chances of being included in either of the groups. This technique ensures that both the groups are identical at the baseline and there is no pre-fixed condition that may influence the variables in question. However, it is mentioned earlier that random assignment of participants in to experimental and control groups is sometimes impractical and unethical in developmental studies. This situation occurs mostly when the variable in question is something that is an innate characteristic, e.g., age, sex, ordinal position of individual etc. In such cases, the researchers resort to another technique known as quasi-experimental method, in which manipulation of variables is made but there is no random assignment of participants. For example, a developmentalist intends to study the causal relationship between ordinal position and personality traits of children in a family. Here, the researcher cannot design a true experimental method because the random assignment of participants into experimental group is not possible, since the ordinal position of the participants is pre-determined based on their order of birth in the family. As such, the researcher would employ quasi experimental method and test the personality traits of the participants with respect to their natural ordinal position.

In this way, quasi experiments are employed when the researcher is interested in independent variables that cannot be randomly assigned. But, as because the participants are not randomly assigned, it is likely that the experimental and control groups are different in baseline with respect to so many other aspects which are not in question in the study but might influence the variable in question and mess-up with results. Thus, quasi-experimental method fails to eliminate the effects of intervening variables and as such, lacks internal validity.

DEVELOPMENTAL OR GENETIC METHODS

Since development is a continuous process, it is necessary to understand how individuals change and develop as they age or proceed form one developmental stage to another. Consequently, developmental psychologists are concerned with the measurement of changes as well differences with respect to different domains of behaviour over age and time. To accomplish this, they adopt three approaches namely longitudinal method, cross-sectional method, and sequential method.

Longitudinal Method

Longitudinal method is a research strategy in which the same individual(s) is studied periodically as they age, over a long enough period of time, usually several years or more. It measures change over time. By doing so, researchers try to understand the general course and pattern of developmental changes across some period of time. For example, if a researcher intends to know how emotional development occurs from infancy to adolescence, he/she would take an infant as subject and study emotional behaviour periodically at the ages of 2, 5, 12, 15 and 18, for example. It is obvious that the investigator using this approach adopts different techniques like experiments, observation, questionnaire, standardized tests etc. Such periodical assessment of emotional behaviour of the same child would give vital information about the change and stability in emotional behaviour. In this way longitudinal method provides a picture of continuous growth and development in different domains. The common domains of development in the study of which longitudinal methods are adopted include locomotion, language and vocabulary, interests, adjustment etc.

Though, longitudinal method provides a continuous picture of development, it has its own drawbacks. It is expensive and time consuming. It requires tremendous investment of time, since the investigator must wait for the participants to age. Furthermore, there is a possibility that a participant may drop out from the study after some stages; may unavailable for later observation or testing because of their flight from the place of residence, getting sick, losing interest or even death. Since the same individual is tested repeatedly, there is again possibility that the participant become familiar with the test and as such perform better in every subsequent testing.

Cross-Sectional Method

To overcome the problem of long await involved in longitudinal method, developmentalists adopt another method known as cross-sectional method. In this method same individual is not studied over different time-spans, rather children of different ages are studied at the same point in time. It may include 3 or 4 groups of children of different ages e.g., 5 years old, 8 years old, and 12 years old and collect data from all the groups simultaneously with respect to dependent variables like memory, vocabulary, locomotion, interests etc. Thus, cross sectional method provides information about differences in development between different age groups within a very short time.

A developmentalist, for instance, intending to know how emotional development occurs from infancy to adolescence, instead of using a longitudinal approach and observing or testing emotional behaviour of the same child periodically at the ages of 2, 5, 12, 15 and 18; might conduct the study simultaneously and observe or test the emotional behaviour of five groups of children belonging to five different age groups- 2 years old, 5 years old, 12 years old, 15 years old and 18 years old, for example, and then compare these groups in terms of emotional behaviour pattern. Thus, cross-sectional study is more economical in terms of time than longitudinal method.

Despite the advantage that a researcher does not have to wait for the participant to grow up or become elder, cross-sectional method brings its own set of difficulties. It entirely ignores the Cohort-Effects. A cohort is a group of people who are born around same time and same place. As such, it is obvious that a particular cohort shares different experiences than other cohorts. For example, individuals born during 1990 in India may expose to a particular environment and share experiences accordingly, which might be different from the experiences shared by individuals who are born during 2010. Therefore, in cross-sectional study if we find that people of different ages; as in our previous instance- 2 years old, 5 years old, 12 years old, 15 years old and 18 years old; differ in emotional behaviour, it may be due to differences in cohort membership and not because of age. Moreover, the cross-sectional method cannot give any information about the consequences of age changes and how individual remain stable throughout ages, since it does not test the individual repeatedly, rather it only talks about age differences in development i.e., the increases and decreases of development.

Sequential Method

It is seen that both the longitudinal and cross-sectional methods have their own drawbacks. The longitudinal method helps in understanding the consequences of age changes but it is time-consuming, whereas the cross-sectional method, though not time consuming, could not help in understanding the consequences of age changes, rather helps only in figuring out the age differences. To overcome these difficulties, researchers often resort to another method known as sequential method which is nothing but a combination of both.

In sequential method developmentalists examine different age groups at several points of time. For example, if a researcher intends to investigate the emotional development of children, he/she would start a cross-sectional approach and examine the emotional behaviour of three or four groups of children of different ages- three years old, four years old and five years old, for example. However, the study would not stop here, rather a longitudinal approach would be started and the emotional behaviour of all the groups would be examined periodically for several years. Subsequently, the three years old group would be examined at the age of three, four and five. The four-year-old group would be examined at the age of four, five and six. Similarly, the five-year-old group would be examined at the age of five, six and seven. Thus, sequential method combines the longitudinal and cross-sectional method and thereby helps in understanding both, the age differences in development as well as consequences of age changes.

PSYCHOANALYTIC METHODS

The psychoanalytic method, as the term implies, is an analysis of psychological state of individuals. It is used in understanding the causes of behavioural abnormalities of individuals. Sigmund Freud, the father of psychoanalysis, started using this method. This method assumes that the root causes of individual's abnormal and maladjusted behaviour lie in the unfulfilled wishes and desires which are repressed in unconscious mind, and as such a careful examination of these latent desires and feelings would help in understanding the nature and causes of maladjusted behaviour. Thus, psychoanalytic technique aims at finding out the root causes of behavioural problems of individuals.

In psychoanalysis, two methods are generally employed namely *dream analysis* and *free association*. In dream analysis the participant is asked to give a detailed description of their dreams, which are then analysed by psychoanalysts to figure out the frustrated desires. In free association, the psychologist talks with the patient about the patient's feelings and difficulties and goes on recording the important points, which are then analysed. However, before starting both the process i.e., dream analysis and free association, establishing rapport with the patient is very crucial. For this, the psychologist makes attempts to let the patient feel at ease and that the psychologist is only his/her friend and well-wisher. The psychologist does not show any undue curiosity to know things about the patient, rather offers a comfortable seat to the patient and encourages to express his/her feelings as he/she wants.

Thus, the psychoanalytic methods make attempts to explore the inner depths of unconscious mind to understand the root causes of maladaptive behaviour. The use of this method is unavoidable in certain circumstances. In fact, there is no other method which can be useful in figuring out the root causes of maladaptive behaviour. However, this method has some limitations. At times, the patient or participant may feel resistance within and stop revealing his/her latent desires and feelings. Second, the conduct of psychoanalysis requires expertise. Only a specially trained psychologist can conduct the psychoanalysis. Finally, this method is time consuming and quite expensive too.

ETHICAL STANDARDS OF RESEARCH IN DEVELOPMENTAL PSYCHOLOGY

The developmental psychologists, while studying individuals, must protect participant's physical as well as psychological wellbeing and safeguard their rights. In order to understand the causal impact of parent's marital violence on children's behaviour, for example, no researcher can put a child in an environment where parents create violence all the time. It would be unethical as it is psychologically harmful for the child. In this way, there are several areas of investigation where developmental psychologists encounter ethical questions. However, research in all the areas of human development is essential to make progress in understanding developmental processes. Therefore, in order to help researchers to avoid such ethical questions, the major organizations of developmentalists like American Psychological Association (APA), The Society for Research in Child Development (SRCD) etc. have developed comprehensive ethical guidelines that need to be followed. The American Psychological Association (APA) in its New Ethical Principles of Psychologists and Code of Conduct updated in 2003 forwarded some principles to be followed in studying children, including freedom from harm, informed consent, the use of deception, maintenance of participant's privacy etc. The Society for Research in Child Development (SRCD) have identified 16 ethical principles for research with children, the details of which can be retrieved from www.srcd.org. For convenience of the readers, a few important ethical guidelines are mentioned below.

1. Protecting participants from physical and psychological harm

The investigator should not use any research procedure that may harm the child either physically or psychologically. The investigator is also always obliged to use the least stressful research procedure wherever possible. The participant's welfare, rights and interests should always be given priority.

2. Obtaining informed consent from the participants

The researcher must obtain consent from the participants, preferably in written form, before starting the experiment. If the participants are over the age of seven, they must voluntarily agree to participate in the study. In case the participants are below 18 years old, their parents or guardians must also provide consent. In the process of obtaining voluntary consent, the researcher should inform the child and guardians about all features of the study that may affect their willingness to participate and should answer all their questions, if any, in terms appropriate to their comprehension.

3. The use of deception must accompany justification and cause no harm to the child

Although full disclosure of all the features of the study should be made to the participants before seeking their consent, some studies may require withholding certain information or use deception. However, such use of deception must go scrutiny by independent panel and must ensure no harm to the child and his/her family. However, as the study completes, all such withholding information should be described and explained to the child and adequate measures to be taken to ensure that the participant understands the reasons for using deception.

4. Maintaining privacy of the participants

The investigator should keep in confidence all the information obtained about research participants. The participant's identity should be concealed in written and verbal reports of the results as well as in informal discussions. If the participant is audio-taped or video-taped, their access to third party must be restricted.

5. Informing participants about their performance

Once the study completes, the investigator should inform the participants about their performance in terms appropriate to their understanding. The investigator also holds a duty to clarify the research participants about any misconceptions that may have arisen during the conduct of the study.

4

Beginning of Life: The Conception

INTRODUCTION

Like all other living species, human beings are also capable of producing its own species through a process called reproduction. The reproduction or the beginning of a new life is the result of union and fertilization of the female reproductive cell by the male reproductive cell. Before proceeding to describe how the reproductive cells of male and female unites, gets fertilized and results in conception, it would be wise to present a structural representation of these two reproductive cells and the process of their formation and maturation.

MALE REPRODUCTIVE CELL: STRUCTURE AND FORMATION

The male reproductive cell is known as *spermatozoa* (spermatozoon in singular form). It is a highly specialised, free swimming and actively motile cell. It is elongated in shape and consists of a head, a neck, a middle piece and a principal piece or tail. It is one of the smallest cells found in human body and the whole length of a spermatozoon from the tip of the head to the end piece of the tail is approximately 55 to 65 micrometres. The head of the spermatozoon consists of 23 highly condensed chromosomes, which is covered with a cap known as *acrosome*, that helps the spermatozoon to penetrate in the female reproductive cell (ovum) during fertilization.

The spermatozoa develop in male reproductive organ known as *testes*. Sperm are produced in winding tubules, within each testis. They are then emptied into the *epididymis*, a long slender, twisted tube, where they are stored. During sexual arousal and ejaculation, the sperm pass from the *epididymis* along muscular ducts into the *urethra*- a tube that connects with the bladder and is surrounded by the man's external reproductive organ, the penis. On the way from *epididymis* to *urethra*, the sperm are mixed with secretions from the *seminal vesicles* and the *prostate gland*. This mixture is called semen. A pair of male *testes* can produce several hundred million spermatozoa in every 4 to 5 days. However, one mature spermatozoon is required for stating of a new life.

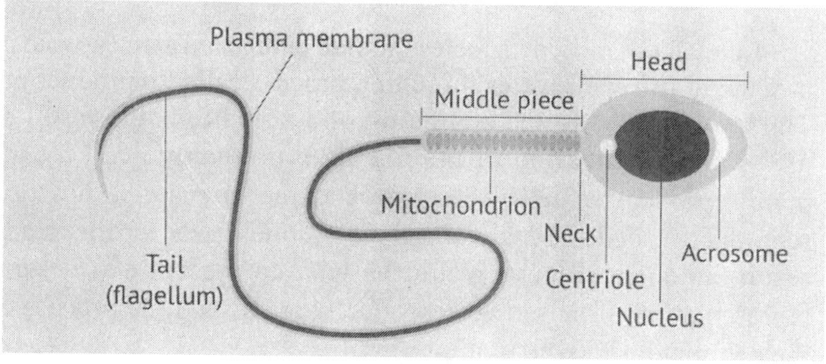

Figure 1: Structure of Spermatozoon. *Source*: www.invtra.com

FEMALE REPRODUCTIVE CELL: STRUCTURE AND FORMATION

The female reproductive cell is known as *ova* (ovum in singular form). It is round shaped and non-motile in structure. It is one of the largest cells found in human body, visible to the naked eye without the aid of a microscope and is approximately .12 millimetre in diameter. Every mature ovum consists of the *nucleus*, the *cytoplasm* (yolk) and the cellular *membrane*. The nucleus contains 23 matched chromosomes, the cytoplasm (yolk) stores the food and nutrients to nourish fertilized egg and the cellular membrane surrounds the cell from outside. The life-span of ovum is 24 to 48 hours.

The ovum is the matured human reproductive cell which develops from the *primitive germ cells* embedded in the *cortex* in the female reproductive organ known as *ovaries*. Each of the primitive germ cells give rise to several small cells called *oogonia* through repeated divisions. *Oogonia* develops into primary *oocyte* and then into mature *ova*. In every menstrual cycle of approximately 28 days, normally one ovum ripens and released from the follicles of one of the ovaries.

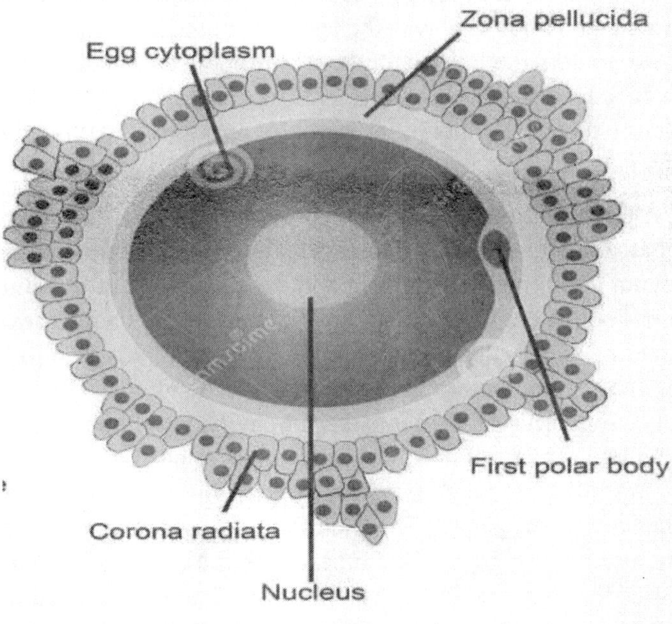

Figure 2: Structure of Ovum. *Source*: www.colorbox.com

THE PROCESS OF FERTILIZATION: THE BEGINNING OF LIFE

Human life begins at fertilization, the process during which a spermatozoon of the male unites with the ovum of the female to form a single cell called *zygote*. This zygote is the beginning of a new life.

In the previous section we discussed how ovum forms and ripens inside the ovaries. In normal circumstances a single mature ovum is released from the follicles of one of the ovaries of a female during each menstrual cycle. This process of releasing or escaping matured ovum from the ovaries during menstrual cycle is called the ovulation process, which occurs during the mid-period of normal menstrual cycle. For example, in a normal cycle of 28 days, the maximum possibility of ovulation is around 14th day of the cycle. However, there are deviations among women with respect to the time of ovulation due to many reasons. Once ovulation occurs, the released ovum finds its way to the open end of the fallopian tube. As the ovum enters the fallopian tube it is propelled along the length of the tube by a combination of agents like cilica, fluids and mucus inside the tube and waits in the *ampulla* region of the tube to get fertilized by spermatozoon.

At this point of time, if there is no supply or availability of spermatozoon by sexual intercourse or any other alternative means, the ovum could not be fertilized and it degenerates after waiting for a period of roughly 24 to 48 hours. However, if there is sexual intercourse during this period of ovulation, hundreds of millions of spermatozoa enter the vagina, from which hundreds of thousand travels through cervix, then into uterine cavity. Few hundred strong spermatozoa then travel up towards the first narrow part of the fallopian tube known as *isthmus*. Among the spermatozoa that reaches *isthmus* region of fallopian tube, few active spermatozoa reach *ampullary* region of the tube where the ovum is waiting to welcome the spermatozoon. Then, the most active, fast, and motile spermatozoon penetrates the wall of the ovum. As the first sperm cell enters the ovum, the surface of the ovum is so changed that no other sperm cell can enter. About one hour or so after the sperm enters the ovum, the two cells suddenly fuse and chromosomes of the sperm cell start forming pairs with the chromosomes of the ovum cell. As a result, a new cell is produced which is known as *zygote*, consisting of 23 pairs of chromosomes- in each pair one from male and one from female. Thus, fertilization is completed when one new cell, known as *zygote*, is produced as a result of the union of sperm cell with the ovum cell and represents the beginning of a new life.

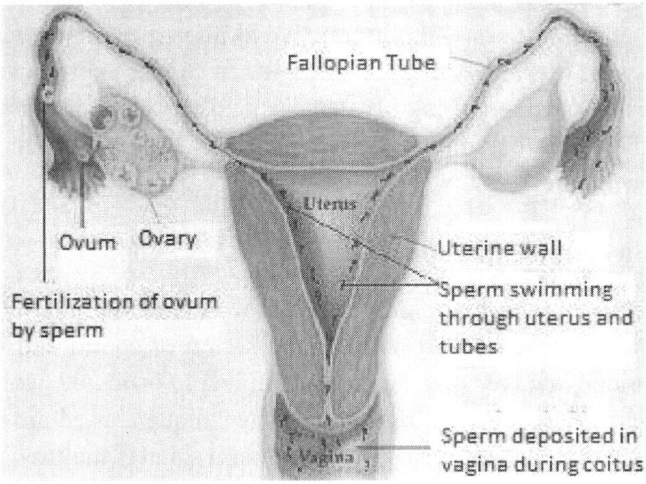

Figure 3: Process of Fertilisation. *Source*: www.healthtree.com

ALTERNATIVE TECHNIQUES OF FERTILIZATION

Problem in fertilization or infertility is a common phenomenon world wide. According to a 2015 Ernst and Young report, 27.5 million couples who are actively seeking children, suffer from infertility in India. According to Indian Society of Assisted Reproduction, infertility affects 10 to 14 percent of the Indian population. Besides medical reasons, modern life style factors like increased marital age, rising tobacco and alcohol consumption, obesity, work stress etc. exert significant negative impact in normal fertilization. The causes of infertility rest with both men and women. In case of women causes like no ovulation or producing abnormal ova, blockage in fallopian tube, degenerative uterus etc. are profound. Among men, factors like low sperm count (mostly less than 15 million per ml), low motility rate of sperm, poor sperm morphology, blocked passageway etc. contribute infertility. In some cases of infertility, surgery may correct the cause, in some others hormone-based drugs may increase the probability of pregnancy, while few cases are not curable. However, recent advancement in biological knowledge has opened new techniques of fertilization. With the use of assisted reproductive technologies, many humans who were previously deemed infertile can choose to produce their own biological offspring instead of adopting a child or remaining childless. Few commonly used techniques of fertilization are given below in brief.

1. Intrauterine Insemination (IUI)

This is the most common type of alternative fertilization technique based on artificial insemination of sperm cells. The technique involves placing sperms artificially inside the women's uterus to facilitate fertilization. This technique is used mostly in case of male infertility caused by low sperm count or motility. When sperm count or motility rate (movement capacity) is poor in men, the ejaculated sperm cells during intercourse are unable to travel up through vagina to uterus to reach the fallopian tube to make the ovum fertile naturally. In such cases, the male sperm cell is collected in laboratory and the concentrated sperm cells are directly inseminated in the uterus with the help of a pipe like device with an aim to increase the number of sperm that reach the fallopian tubes and subsequently increase the chances of fertilization. However, before the intrauterine insemination, medicines are used on female to stimulate ovulation, which is followed by careful monitoring to determine the time of ovum maturation and ovulation. The IUI procedure is then performed around the time of ovulation. It is less invasive and less expensive technique in comparison to in-vitro fertilization technique. However, since ovulation stimulating drugs are used in IUI, there is possibility of more than one ovum getting matured and released from the follicles of one or both the ovaries and as such there is possibility of multiple birth in case of IUI treatment.

2. In-Vitro Fertilization (IVF)

By far the most common high-tech assisted reproduction technique used is *in-vitro fertilization (IVF)*, in which eggs (ova) and sperms are combined and fertilized outside the body, in a laboratory dish. If any egg is successfully fertilized in the laboratory, it is transferred into the women's uterus. The process starts with applying fertility drugs on women followed by monitoring the ovulation process and collecting (retrieving) matured ovum from the ovaries. Afterwards, the collected ovum is combined with the sperm in a liquid in a dish in laboratory setting. Once the ovum in the dish is fertilised, the zygote or fertilized egg undergoes embryo culture for 2 to 6 days, and is then transferred into the women's uterus with the help of needle like device. The embryo then implants naturally inside women's uterine wall and the women become pregnant. IVF can be used in both male as well as female infertility. In case of female, if there is blocked or damaged fallopian tube or the tube is removed, the natural travel of sperm towards the ovum is disturbed resulting in infertility. Again, ovulation disorders like no ovulation or producing abnormal ova, premature ovarian failure etc. prevents natural fertilization. In case of male, factors like low sperm count or low motility rate decreases the chances of fertilization. In all such cases, IVF can be effectively employed. However, there is possibility of multiple births as a result of fertilization techniques including *in-vitro fertilization*. Studies have also shown that in-vitro fertilization twins have a slight increased risk of low birth weight.

3. Intracytoplasmic Sperm Injection (ICSI)

ICSI is a revolutionary technique used in *in-vitro fertilization*. Generally, in IVF the egg or eggs, after retrieval from the ovaries is allowed to get fertilized with sperm cells in a laboratory dish. However, in traditional or classic IVF, the fertilization of every egg (ovum) needs around 50 to 100 thousand sperm cells, because it needs to perform acrosome reaction which requires the involvement of thousands of sperm. But, *Intracytoplasmic Sperm Injection*

(ICSI) is a procedure of IVF where acrosome reaction is skipped and a single sperm cell is injected directly into every retrieved egg. Hence, there is no need of thousands of sperm against each egg, rather each egg requires a single sperm cell. Once the fertilized egg turns into an embryo of about 8 to 16 cells through embryo culture procedure in the laboratory, it is then placed back in the women's uterus to implant itself. In this process, the sperm may need to be removed from the intending father or the donor using a needle or biopsy. This process of ICSI usually results minor discomfort and have higher success rate.

Thus, with the advancement of science and technology several alternative techniques are in place today that helps in fertilization. Besides the above-mentioned techniques, fertility drugs, donor sperm, surrogacy, donor eggs, reproductive surgery, Gamete Intra fallopian Transfer (GIFT), Zygote Intra fallopian Transfer (ZIFT) etc. are some other alternative techniques used in fertilization. In a technological miracle, Japanese researchers unveiled the first artificial 'womb tank' in 1997, a technological wonder that could potentially revolutionize the bearing of children and child birth in coming years.

CONDITIONS DETERMINED AT THE TIME OF FERTILIZATION

The stage of fertilization is very crucial for a new-born baby. During this stage some conditions get fixed which have significant impact in the future development and which cannot be replaced in later stages of life. During the fertilization process when the chromosomes from both the cells (spermatozoon and ovum) starts mingling with each other and form pairs, the sex of the new child is determined, hereditary characteristics received from each parent is set and a new life begins. E. Hurlock in her book on Child Development had mentioned four conditions determined during fertilization which has far reaching and long-lasting effects on the individual's future development. These are given briefly as below.

1. Fixation of Heredity Endowment

What heredity endowments the prospective individual will inherit from his parents and forefathers is determined at the time of fertilization. The moment when a sperm cell unites with the ovum cell, the genetic contribution is fixed, which cannot be changed or modified later. The sperm and ovum involved in fertilization (each containing 23 unpaired chromosomes alongside thousands of genes) creates a unique combination of genetic code out of trillions of possible combinations. This unique genetic combination occurred by chance determines most physical and mental traits of an individual. Hence, had there been a different gamete (sperm or ovum) involved in fertilization, or had there been a different combination of genetic code occurred during gametes formation, the individual would have been completely different. And neither the gametes nor the genetic combinations can be changed once fertilization occurred. Thus, whatever the heredity endowment is, it is fixed at the moment of fertilization.

2. Determination of Sex

Whether the prospective baby will be a boy or girl is fixed at the time of fertilization. The fertilized egg consists of 23 pairs of chromosomes, in each pair one contributed by each of the parents. Out of these, the first 22 pairs are called *autosomes,* which are similar in size and shape and carries all the heredity endowments. The 23rd pair (one each from each parent) is called *sex chromosome* that determines the sex of the baby. This 23rd chromosome is different in shape and size between male and female. For male's sperm it is of two types- X-shaped, which is large in size and Y shaped, which is smaller. On the contrary, female's ovum has only X shaped 23rd chromosome, which is large in size and does not have Y shaped chromosome at all. As such, during fertilization, if the sperm of male containing X-shaped 23rd chromosome unites with the ovum of female, the combination of 23rd pair of chromosomes will be XX, resulting in birth of a girl child. On the other hand, if sperm containing Y shaped 23rd chromosome unites with the ovum, the combination will be XY, which always gives birth to girl child. Thus, the sex of the individual is fixed just at the moment of fertilization that cannot be changed later.

3. Number of Offspring

Number of offspring to be born at a time, is fixed at the time of fertilization or right after fertilization. The women may conceive twins, triplets, quadruplets or so on. Customarily, one ovum is released from one of the ovaries during a menstrual cycle which is then fertilized by a sperm cell, resulting in birth of a single baby (singleton). However, if more than one ovum is released in a menstrual cycle, all or some of them may be fertilized by sperm cells and the result will be multiple embryos in the uterus. This process of multiple births is called *dizygotic, trizygotic* etc. depending upon the number of ova fertilized. As such, how many babies will get birth depends upon how many matured ova is released and how many of them are successfully fertilized. Thus, number of offspring is fixed at fertilization. However, sometimes it is also fixed right after fertilization. This mechanism is called as *monozygotic*, where the ovum just after fertilization may split into separate parts (mostly splits into two parts; in very rare cases into three or more), which then nourish separately and gives birth to multiple births depending on the number of splits. The detailed mechanisms of multiple births are discussed later in chapter 5.

4. Ordinal Position in the Family

The ordinal position means the child's position in the sequence of siblings in the family. Right at the moment of fertilization or conception the prospective child takes certain position in the family's hierarchy. He/she becomes the first child or middle child, or second child the youngest child or so on. This ordinal position fixed at fertilization exerts a significant influence in later stages of life. It determines what relationships, roles, and responsibilities he/she would have with other members, which have a profound significance in his developmental process.

Because of all the fixations and determination, the moment of fertilization is treated as one of the most crucial in human life.

5

Genetic Foundations of Life: The Genes and Chromosomes

INTRODUCTION

So far in the previous chapter it is explained that life starts out of a single cell (zygote) formed as a result of fertilization of the egg by the sperm cell. Each fertilized egg contains 46 chromosomes in 23 pairs; in each pair one chromosome form father and one from mother. Chromosomes are long threadlike structures made up of *Deoxyribonucleic Acid* (DNA). DNA is a complex molecule with a structure of a spiral staircase that contains genetic information. Small segments of DNA are called genes. Thus, genes are the units of genetic information, which direct cells to reproduce themselves and assemble proteins for maintaining life.

The 23 pairs of chromosomes of a fertilized egg contain around 25000 genes. These 46 chromosomes (23 pairs) along with 25000 genes, consists of genetic foundation that guides all the future cell activity for the rest of the individual's life. The inherited genetic information orchestrates and determines the growth from a single cell (zygote) weighing about twenty millionth of an ounce to a person made of trillions of cells. The proceeding sections describe how genetic inheritance determines the foundations of life.

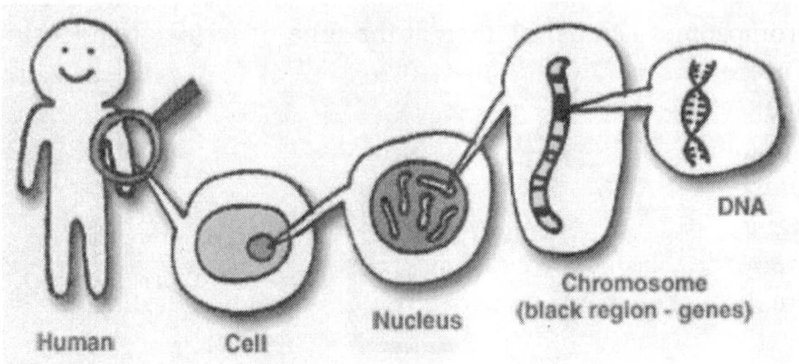

Figure 4: Genetic Material.

Source: www.ashg.com

Note: One Human Cell = 23 Chromosome Pairs = 46 Chromosomes = 25000 Genes = Total Genetic Foundation

HOW FAR GENETIC INHERITANCE MAKES AN INDIVIDUAL UNIQUE?

So far it is known that each fertilized egg contains 23 pairs of chromosomes, 23 from father and 23 from mother. If each parent provides just 23 chromosomes, why do we find vast diversity of human beings? Or why are siblings so different? To answer these questions, it is important to understand the process of cell division of gametes- ovum or spermatozoon.

All the cells in human body, except gametes (ova or sperm), have 46 chromosomes arranged in 23 pairs, in each pair one from father and one from mother. All the cells, except gametes (ova or sperm), are formed through a process called *mitosis*, during which each chromosome in the original cell (46 in number) duplicates itself and thus produces 92 chromosomes. Afterwards, the cell divides into two, each containing 46 chromosomes (23 pairs). Thus, at the end of mitosis each of the two new cells contains 23 pairs of chromosomes with the same DNA as original cell called *diploid*.

But, in case of the formation of gametes (sperm and ova) the process of mitosis is not followed. Because, if gametes (sperm or ovum) are formed using *mitosis*, each new cell will have 46 chromosomes (23 pairs), then at the time of fertilization (fusion of sperm and ovum cell), the zygote will have 92 chromosomes, which is abnormal. Hence, the gametes are formed in human body through a more complex kind of process called *meiosis*. During *meiosis*, members of each pair of chromosomes (23 pairs) in the original cell in testes or in ovaries are separated and get duplicated, hereby produce 92 chromosomes. But afterwards, the cell divides twice, thus forming four cells, each of which has only half of the genetic material of the original cell (diploid). Thus, at the end of the meiosis, each sperm or ovum has 23 unpaired chromosomes.

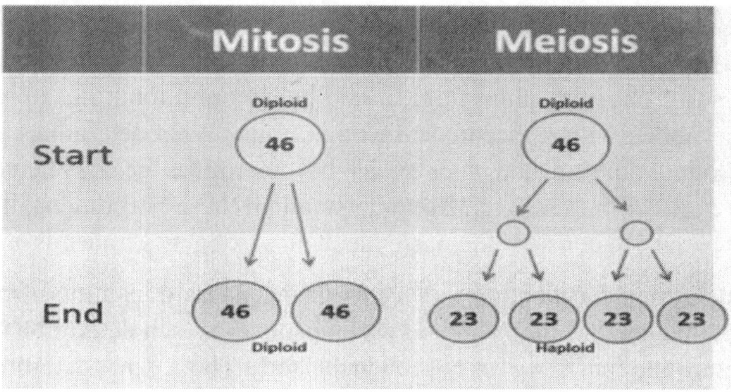

Figure 5: Process of Fertilisation.

Source: www.youtube.com

Since at the time of the gamete (sperm or ovum) formation through meiosis, the members of each pair of chromosomes in the original cell (diploid) in testes or ovaries are separated, which chromosome in the pair go to the gamete (sperm or ovum) is only a matter of chance. Because of the chance factor of chromosome contribution to the gamete, there are some 8 million different combinations possible. In addition, before the pair separates, pieces of the two chromosomes in each pair are exchanged, creating a new combination of genes on each chromosome. Thus, when chromosomes from the mother's egg and father's sperm are brought together in the zygote, the result is a truly unique combination of genes. There are tens of trillions of possible genetic combinations.

Because so many combinations are provided by genetic inheritance, there is no likelihood of genetic duplication of two individuals, except identical twins.

HOW FAR GENETIC INHERITANCE DETERMINES OBSERVABLE TRAITS?

We know that the offspring inherits genetic information from both the parents in the form of genes and chromosomes. If, as we know, both the parents transmit equal number of chromosomes (23) to the offspring, then why does the new-born individual, sometimes, resemble either father or mother, or resemble both but in different magnitude; or why does he/she resemble to father with respect to some physical, physiological and behavioural traits and to his/her mother with respect to some other traits? What determines the colour of our skin, hair, eyes etc.? What determines the body height, strength of muscles etc.? To understand all these phenomena, it is necessary to consider the basic mechanism of genes transmission.

During fertilization thousands of genes are transmitted from both the parents alongside 46 chromosomes, which determine the nature and function of every cell in the body. These genes determine which cells will ultimately become part of the heart and which will become part of the muscles of the leg. They also determine how different parts of the body will function, for instance, how rapidly the heart will beat or how strength a muscle will have. These genes occur in pairs, one on a maternal chromosome and other on the corresponding paternal chromosome. A particular trait or characteristic of an individual is the result of any two genes in pair (one member of the pair of genes is called an allele). Though, for a particular trait or characteristic the new-born carries genes from both the parents- one *allele* from father and one *allele* from mother, both cannot be expressed. Some alleles are of *dominant* in nature while some alleles are *recessive*. The dominant allele completely masks or hides the recessive allele, and only the dominant trait gets expressed. As such, the observable trait of the newly born individual is the result of dominant allele.

The mechanism will become clear, if we consider a particular trait, for instance, the eye colour. The eye colour of the individual is determined by two genes in pair- one allele from father and one allele from mother. If the allele contributed by the father is dominant in nature and the father is black eyed, and the allele contributed by the mother is recessive and the mother is brown eyed, then the dominant trait will be expressed in the offspring. That means the eye colour of the newly created individual will become black. On the contrary, if the allele contributed by mother is dominant then the individual will become brown eyed.

Because of this mechanism of genes transmission, an individual sometimes resembles his/her father with respect to some traits and mother with respect to some other traits. We often observe that an individual's eye colour resembles his father's eye colour while his/her face structure resembles his/her mother's face. All such variations occur as a result of dominant and recessive nature of genes.

However, it is not to be mistaken that the genetic materials related to only dominant allele remain present in an individual and genetic material related to recessive allele are not, just because the dominant traits are expressed externally and recessive traits are not. Rather, the genetic materials from both the allele (one each from each of the parents) is present in the offspring, even though not expressed (displayed) externally. The underlying combination of genetic material present (but not visible externally or outwardly) in an organism is called *Genotype*, while the externally observable traits and characteristics like physical, physiological, and behavioural traits are called *Phenotype*. Thus, *genotype* is the result of recessive allele while the *phenotype* is the result of dominant allele.

HOW DOES GENETIC INHERITANCE DETERMINE SEX OF THE OFFSPRING?

Historically and even today many societies prefer the birth of a male child rather than female due to many social stereotypes.

Before the advent of genetic studies women were considered responsible for determining the gender of the offspring. There are many evidences showing how women are faulted, divorced, and even killed for not producing male child. However, the advancement of genetic study has revealed that it is the male not the female responsible for determining sex of the offspring. To understand how an offspring turned a boy or a girl, it is necessary to consider the nature of chromosomes in both male's sperm and female's ovum.

We know that a fertilized egg (zygote) consists of 23 pairs of chromosomes, 23 provided by father and 23 provided by mother. Of these, the first 22 chromosomes transmitted by male and the first 22 chromosomes transmitted by female are similar in size and shape. These chromosomes are called *autosomes* and are responsible for determining most of the traits of the individual. The 23rd pair of chromosomes (one each from father and mother) is called *sex chromosome* that determines the sex of the individual. Unlike the first 22 pair of chromosomes, there is differences between male and female with respect to the 23rd chromosome. With respect to male sperm, the 23rd chromosome is of two types. The X shaped and Y shaped. The X shaped chromosome is larger in size, while the Y shaped chromosome is smaller in size. But, in case of female ovum, the 23rd chromosome is only X shaped, and large in-size. There is no Y shaped sex chromosome in female. Consequently, so far the 23rd chromosome is concerned, by default the female ovum transmits X chromosome, while the male sperm may either transmit X or Y chromosome. If the male sperm transmits X, it will make pair with X chromosome in female ovum, and the fertilized egg will have XX pairing on the 23rd chromosome, which will always produce a female offspring. On the contrary, if the male sperm transmits Y chromosome, it will make pair with X chromosome in female ovum, and the fertilized ovum will have XY combination on the 23rd chromosome- result will be a male offspring. In this way, the 23rd chromosome in the father's sperm determines the sex of the offspring.

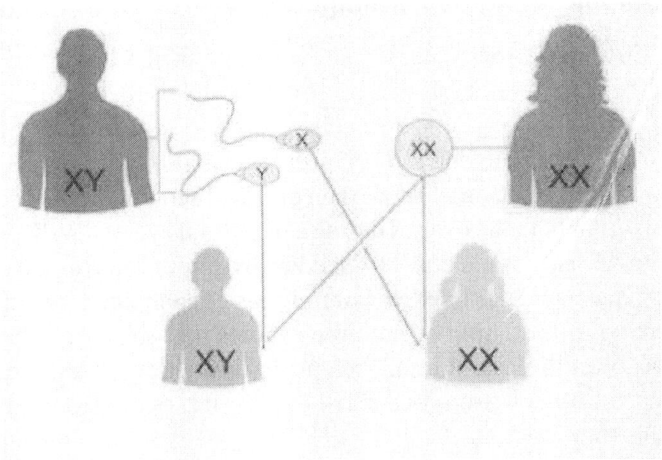

Figure 6: 23rd chromosome of male and female gametes determining sex.

HOW DOES GENETIC INHERITANCE CONTRIBUTE TO MULTIPLE BIRTHS?

Multiple births generally refer to the birth of two or more babies within a few hours or days. If two children born together, they are called twins, in case of three they are called triplets, and quadruplets is called when four babies born together. There are evidences of a greater number of multiple births. However, among multiple births, the birth of two babies (twins) is more common in comparison to other types. Meredith, H.V. in Hurlock, E.(1997) reported that twins occur in every 80 births, triplets once in every 9000 births, and quadruplets once in every 570000 births. What makes such multiple births? Is there any genetic contribution of multiple births? Questions like these can be answered by understanding the mechanism of multiple births.

There are two mechanisms of multiple births- (a) Multiple births from multiple zygotes and (b) Multiple births from single zygote. Let us understand the mechanisms.

1. Multiple Births from Multiple Zygotes

Customarily in a menstrual cycle, one of the two ovaries of women matures and releases one ovum which is then fertilized by one of the millions of sperm cells, resulting in formation of one zygote that subsequently gives birth to a single child (singletons). However, in some cases more than one ovum matures and releases from one or both the ovaries during a menstrual cycle. If so happens, all the released ovum may be fertilized by sperm cells (as we know that male ejaculates hundreds of millions of sperm cells at a time), resulting in formation of multiple zygotes that subsequently give birth to multiple children. Except the influence of fertilization drugs, the other reasons of such multiple releases of ova are mostly unknown.

Thus, if a woman releases two ova in a cycle, two separate zygotes will form, that will give birth to two babies. Twins born through this process is called *dizygotic twins*, since they are born from two different zygotes. Such twins are genetically different from one another and as such one may be boy and another may be girl or both may be of same sex. Since, they both inherit different genetic information, they are non-identical and hence are called *fraternal* twins. Similarly, if a woman releases three ova simultaneously in a cycle, three different zygotes may form and the woman will give birth to three genetically non-identical babies, all of them may be of same or different sex. The triplets born through this process is called *trizygotic triplets*, since they are born from three different zygotes.

2. Multiple Births from Single Zygote

In some cases, though initially a single *zygote* is formed as a result of fertilization of a single ovum by a sperm cell, yet at a later stage during the cell division process, the zygote splits into multiple parts (mostly two) instead of remaining together. These separate divisions of the same zygote then nourish separately and subsequently give birth to multiple babies. Except the evidence of hormonal disturbances, the other certain causes of such separation are not known.

Thus, if the zygote during the cell division process splits into two, the result is the birth of two children. Twins born through this process is called *monozygotic twins* as they are originally born from a single zygote. Such twins are genetically identical and as such both are of the same sex. Since, they both inherit same genetic information, they are identical in all respects and hence are also called *identical* twins. Similarly, if the zygote splits into three parts or initially splits into two parts and one of them splits again into two; the result will be the birth of three babies with the same genetic inheritance. Triplets born through this process are known as *monozygotic triplets* and are of same sex. However, the monozygotic triplets are very rare. Babies born through this mechanism, whether they are monozygotic twins or monozygotic triplets or more, are completely identical in all respects and any change among them in future is attributed to environmental influences.

It needs to understand that twins may occur through any one of the above mentioned two mechanisms at a time- either from single zygote (*monozygotic twins)* or from multiple (two) zygotes (*dizygotic twins)*. However, triplets, quadruplets, quintuplets and even more births may be produced by either of the mechanism or by both the mechanisms at a time. Triplets, for instance, may occur from a single zygote (*monozygotic triplets*), or from multiple (three) zygotes (*trizygotic triplets*). However, triplets may also be *dizygotic*- one baby from one zygote and the other two babies from another zygote.

The possibilities of multiple births are less in case of natural fertilization. It increases with adoption of fertilization treatment. The fertility drugs applied on women stimulate the ova maturation process. As a result, occasionally, not universally, one or both the ovaries release multiple matured ova in a menstrual cycle resulting in multiple births. Research on Caucasian couples in United States showed that 1 in every 10 couples who used fertility drugs have dizygotic twins, compared to overall figure of 1 dizygotic twin in every 86 couples. Moreover, multiple births are more common in *in-vitro fertilization* (IFV). In IVF several ova are fertilized in dishes in laboratory. To increase the chances of successful implantation in uterine wall, several fertilized ova are inserted in the uterus. This, sometimes results in multiple successful implantations, resulting in multiple births. Besides, increase of maternal age is also positively correlated with chances of multiple births.

GENETIC DISORDERS

Genes and chromosomes, the foundations of life, sometimes are responsible for occurrence of certain disorders which are hard to cure at later stages of development. Every couple, particularly those worrying about the chances of conceiving child with genetic and chromosomal abnormalities, should be aware of all such possible disorders and the procedures of their early diagnosis and intervention before it goes out of hand.

Some disorders are caused by abnormalities in the whole chromosome (uneven number of chromosomes, instead of normal 23 pairs), while some others are caused by harmful genes in the chromosomes. Let us discuss the common disorders caused by chromosomal abnormalities as well as gene abnormalities.

DISORDERS ASSOCIATED WITH CHROMOSOMAL ABNORMALITIES

We know that in normal cases, a zygote is formed with 23 pair of chromosomes (23 from father's sperm and 23 from mother's ovum). But, in some cases the sperm or the ovum carries less or a greater number of chromosomes, rather than 23. The zygote formed with such sperm and ovum having abnormal number of chromosomes may lead to certain disorders, mostly of two types (a) Down Syndrome and (b) Sex linked chromosomal disorders.

1. Down Syndrome

The most common disorder associated with chromosomal abnormalities is known as *down syndrome.* It is a mental retardation that occurs as a result of one extra copy in the 21st pair of chromosomes. A normal baby gets birth out of 23 pairs of chromosomes; in each pair one chromosome is contributed by each of the parents. In cases of *down syndrome*, there are three copies of 21st chromosome. Due to one extra copy of 21st chromosome, the total chromosome stands at 47, instead of usual 46. The additional 21st chromosome, though may be contributed by either of the parents, 95 % chances lie with the mother. The excess genetic material in the form of additional 21st chromosome alters the normal course of development and causes the symptoms of *down syndrome*. The common characteristics of individuals with down syndrome include round face, flattened skull, an extra fold of skin over the eyelids, short limbs, retardation of motor skills, mental retardation of mild to moderate level etc. The down syndrome caused by three copies of 21st chromosome is medically known as *Trisomy 21* and 95% cases of down syndrome belong to this category. There is other two types of down syndrome which are very rare. These are *translocation* and *mosaicism*. In *translocation*, an extra part of the 21st chromosome gets stuck onto another chromosome. It occurs in about 3-4% of people with down syndrome. In *mosaicism*, the person with down syndrome has an extra 21st chromosome in only some of the cells but not all of them. 1-2 % of people with down syndrome are of this type. Irrespective of type of down syndrome, every affected child develops differently. According to the World Health Organisation (WHO), the estimated incidence of down syndrome worldwide is between 1 in 1,000 to 1 in 1,100 live births.

The causes of down syndrome are still unknown. Research indicates that older mother has a high possibility of having a child with down syndrome. Parents of a child with down syndrome suffer from high risk of giving birth to another child with down syndrome, with chances of approximately 1 in 100 (Down Syndrome Federation of India).

There are several prenatal diagnostic tests like *Chorionic Villus Sampling* (CVS), *Amniocentesis, Triple Screen* (a type of maternal blood test), *Non-invasive Prenatal Diagnosis* (NIPD) etc. for detecting down syndrome in the mother's womb. However, there are ethical questions about whether the couple should opt for pregnancy termination or not, if down syndrome is identified after undergoing prenatal diagnostic tests. It is not always that children born with down syndrome becomes parasite and cannot participate in social life. Though there is no cure of the disorder, the early intervention services like routine medical care, involvement in school and community activities, support from parents and community members can help children with down syndrome to develop social skills and adapt successfully to the environment. Today, with the advancement of medical sciences and a better understanding of the disorder, the life expectancy of people with down syndrome have gone up to 50 years. There are instances of adults with down syndrome getting married and forming their own families. However, the children of parents with down syndrome have 50% chance of having normal intelligence (NDSS, 2007).

2. Sex Linked Chromosomal Disorders

Besides *down syndrome* that occurs as a result of abnormalities in 21st chromosome, the other chromosome related disorders are associated with abnormalities in the 23rd pair of chromosomes. Since, 23rd pair of chromosome determines the sex of the offspring, the disorders associated with this are often called *sex linked chromosomal abnormalities*. There may be four types of sex chromosome related disorders. These are given below.

a. ***Klinefelter Syndrome:*** This syndrome occurs among male as a result of one extra X chromosome. In normal cases, the pair of 23rd or sex chromosome is XY, X contributed by mother and Y contributed by father. But in case of Klinefelter Syndrome, the offspring (male) inherits one additional X chromosome, making the pair XXY instead of XY. Thus, the total number of chromosomes in each cell becomes 47 instead of usual 46. The additional genetic material in the form of one extra X chromosome affects normal development and results in abnormalities in physical, sexual, and intellectual development. Males with Klinefelter syndrome typically have small testes that produces reduced amount of testosterone which leads to delayed or incomplete sexual development. Other symptoms include enlarged breast, less body hair, reduced muscle mass, reduced sperm production etc. Due to low testosterone, males with this syndrome often cannot become biological father without the help of assisted reproductive technologies.

b. ***The XYY Syndrome*:** The XYY syndrome is just opposite to Klinefelter syndrome, which occurs in males as a result of one extra Y chromosome, making the combination of 23rd pair of chromosomes XYY, rather than usual XY. Thus, like Klinefelter syndrome, here also the total number of chromosomes in each cell of the body becomes 47 instead of 46, with one extra Y chromosome in 23rd pair. This condition is sometimes called *Jacob's syndrome, XYY Karyotype* or *YY syndrome.* The symptoms include weak muscle tone, delayed motor skill, speech difficulties, learning disabilities, taller than average etc.

c. ***Turner Syndrome (TS)*:** Turner syndrome is a chromosomal disorder in females, where they are born either with only one X chromosome or with part of one X chromosome being missed, making the person X0, instead of usual XX. The total number of chromosomes in the cells of females with Turner syndrome, thus becomes either 45 or 45 plus 1 partially missing chromosome, rather than complete 46. Females with Turner syndrome have short stature and a webbed neck. There is loss of ovarian function that contributes to infertility among females with this disorder.

d. ***Fragile X Syndrome (FXS)*:** This syndrome occurs as a result of breakdown of X chromosome. Though found in both males and females, males are more prone to Fragile X syndrome, because the combination of sex chromosome in female is XX. If one X chromosome breaks the other X counteracts the loss. But in case of male such compensation is not possible since the combination is XY. The prominent symptoms of this syndrome include mental retardation, learning disabilities, abnormal physical features like long and narrow face, large ears, flexible fingers, large testicles etc.

The Sex-linked chromosomal disorders are most often remains unidentified until adulthood. It is when people visit physician to treat infertility due to reduced sperm count (in males) or ovarian difficulties (in females), they may be diagnosed as having sex linked chromosomal disorders. Lab tests, imaging techniques and chromosome analysis may be performed to confirm the type of disorders. Though not curable, the symptoms and effects of sex-linked chromosomal disorders can be reduced and controlled through hormone therapy (testosterone replacement), genetic counseling and different types of speech and educational therapies.

DISORDERS ASSOCIATED WITH GENES

Not always the inherited disorders are caused by the uneven number of chromosomes; sometimes harmful genes contained in chromosomes also cause inherited disorders. As many as 7,000 disorders caused by defective genes are identified so far. A few common are given below.

1. **Phenylketonuria (PKU):** PKU is a kind of inherited disorder that occurs as a result of recessive gene. Due to the dominance of recessive gene, the body cannot metabolize phenylalanine, an amino acid, which often leads to mental retardation. In case of PKU the function of spinal cord, brain and motor skill is disturbed. Special diet ensuring less quantity of phenylalanine can control the symptoms of PKU.
2. **Sickle Cell Anemia:** This disorder occurs due to impairment of body's red blood cells. In normal cases the shape of red blood cells is like a 'disk' that carries oxygen to the cells of the body. In case of sickle cell anemia, a recessive gene impairs the red blood cells and become hook shaped, 'sickle', that cannot carry adequate oxygen to the cells. As a result, the cells die quickly and anemia occurs. The symptoms of this disorder include poor appetite, stunted growth, swollen stomach, and yellowish eyes. Peoples with sickle cell anemia have very short life span, rarely live beyond childhood.
3. **Tay-Sach Disease:** Some harmful genes the metabolic

disturbances result in Tay-Sach disease. In case of the disorder, a person cannot attend to anything and characterized by lethargy. There is high risk of paralytic stroke of people with this disease. Though medication and special diet are used to reduce symptoms, a child with Tay-Sach disease dies within five years of age.

4. **Spina Bifida:** It is an inherited disorder that results from gene abnormalities. In this case, a portion of neural tube fails to develop properly causing defects in spinal cord, the bones of the spine and in brain. The treatment of spina bifida is mostly done by surgery just after birth.

5. **Cystic Fibrosis:** Cystic fibrosis is a progressive genetic disorder that causes lung infections and limits ability to breath. A defective gene causes buildup of thick and sticky mucus in the lungs that eventually clogs the airways and traps bacteria leading to infections, damage of lungs and respiratory problems. Peoples with cystic fibrosis need to work closely with medical professionals for effective treatments. Treatments include physical and oxygen therapy, synthetic enzymes, and antibiotics. Most people with CF live to middle age.

There are other disorders like Hemophilia, Huntington's disease, Diabetes etc. that are caused by gene abnormalities. As every individual inherits unique genetic code, there are possibilities of inheriting genetic abnormalities causing serious physical malformations and mental disorders. It is not like that every individual who carries some sort of harmful genes suffers from genetic disorders. Sometimes the adverse effects of harmful genetic materials are compensated by other healthy genes and developmental events. Though there is no permanent cure of inherited disorders, the early diagnosis and effective interventions can go a long way in controlling the symptoms and increasing life expectancy of affected people. Today there are so many advanced prenatal diagnostic tests that can detect the possibility of inherited disorders with precision. Ultrasound Sonography, MRI, Chorionic

Villus Sampling (CVS), Amniocentesis, Triple Screen, Noninvasive Prenatal Diagnosis (NIPD) etc. are some of the advanced techniques that a couple may opt during pregnancy.

6

Prenatal Development and the Birth Process

INTRODUCTION

Until recently, development during prenatal period was not comprehensively investigated due to many reasons, though it holds significant bearing on later developments. In recent years with the advent of specialised techniques in medical science, several fascinating studies are being conducted providing detailed information and understanding of the process and milestones of prenatal development. The prenatal period is the time spent in mother's womb between conception and birth. It lasts typically between 266 days to 280 days. The embryologists traditionally divide the prenatal period in to three stages: Germinal stage, Embryonic stage, and Fetal stage. The present chapter discusses the developmental process and milestones across prenatal period and ends with an elaboration of conditions effecting prenatal development along with possible developmental hazards and their preventive measures. A synoptic picture on the process of birth is also sketched.

GERMINAL PERIOD: FROM FERTILIZATION TO TWO WEEKS

The germinal period includes the period starting with the fertilization and lasts till first two weeks in the mother's womb. It is already discussed earlier that life begins with creation of a single celled *zygote* as a result of fertilisation of ovum by the sperm cell in mother's fallopian tube. After fertilization the zygote or the fertilised ovum travels downs the fallopian tube towards the uterus for a period of 3-4 days. Once the zygote (now called *blastocyst* as cell division inside the zygote occurs) enters the uterine cavity, it floats freely for 2-3 days and later started to contact with endometrium (the inner layer of uterus); and subsequently the blastocyst implants itself to the uterine wall. Once the implantation of the blastocyst is complete the germinal period is over. This implantation typically takes place about 11-15 days after fertilization and hence the embryologists define germinal period as the development that takes place in the first two weeks after fertilization.

The development during the germinal period is characterised by two milestones, rapid cell division and differentiation, and implantation of the zygote to the uterine wall. Short after fertilization the single celled zygote starts methodical cell divisions through the process called *mitosis* (refer chapter 5). The single cell splits into two, and then two doubles to four, four to eight, eight to sixteen and so on. Three days after fertilization it consists of some 32 cells and within a week it is made of 100-150 cells. By the time uterine cavity is reached, the cell cluster becomes hollow and fluid-filled and is referred to as *blastocyst*. Approximately one week after fertilisation, the differentiation of cells within the blastocyst begins and three layers of cells are differentiated viz. *ectoderm, endoderm* and *mesoderm* which participate in forming different cells and tissues in later stages. Though rapid cell division and differentiation takes place during germinal period, it is mostly internal and practically unchanged in size because the cell does not receive any external nutrition.

As the organism reaches the uterus, the inner wall of the uterus i.e., endometrium prepares itself to host the blastocyst. The endometrium becomes vascular, glandular, and thick because of hormone *progesterone* released from ovaries. As a result, the organism implants itself in the wall of the uterus and derives nourishment from the eroded tissue and maternal blood flow. In some cases, the organism (blastocyst) could not complete its travel down towards the uterus and gets implanted in the fallopian tube (oviduct). Such pregnancy is known as *Ectopic Pregnancy* and may cause serious complications for the mother if undetected at an early stage. The fallopian tube can burst as the embryo grows larger and can lead to the death of the mother.

EMBRYONIC PERIOD: FROM THE END OF TWO WEEKS TO EIGHT WEEKS

As stated earlier, the germinal period ends as the blastocyst implants to the uterine wall by two weeks. The embryonic period starts subsequently after the blastocyst implants itself in the uterus and continues till the organism develops as a recognisable human fetus, which typically occurs by eight weeks. As such,the time span of the embryonic period starts from the end of two weeks and lasts till the end of eight weeks of pregnancy.

The developing organism in this stage is called an embryo and characterised by (a) rapid growth, (b) development of life support system, and (c) formation of all the chief organs. The growth rate is so fast in embryonic stage that a microscopically small blastocyst, by the end of eight weeks weighs about 1.25 ounce and 2 cm long. Such rapid growth occurs as the embryo gets external nourishment from mother's blood stream. The life support system of the embryo including the amnion, the umbilical cord and the placenta develop rapidly. The amnion and the umbilical cord develop from the embryo whereas the placenta, a type of membrane forms out of combined contribution of the embryo and uterus tissue of the mother. This support system allows the entry of food materials, hormones, oxygen, and other nutrients into the embryo from mother's blood stream and eliminates carbon dioxide and metabolic wastes from the embryo into mother's blood stream.

All the major organs both internal and external are developing now in this stage except the sex organ and the organism becomes like a miniature human being. As stated earlier that three layers of cells viz. ectoderm, endoderm and mesoderm are formed during the end of germinal period, now participates in the formation of different cells and tissues during the embryonic stage. The ectoderm cells eventually form the skin, the lungs, and the nervous system; the endoderm cells form the lining of the digestive tract, the liver and other associated digestive organs; while the mesoderm cells give rise to the heart and kidneys, blood cells, bones, muscles, and tendons.

By 21 to 25 days, the embryo's heart is developed and starts beating. Hand and trunk appear and tiny arm buds begin to form, followed by leg buds. Other internal organs are present in simple form and functions as they grow. By 30 days, the embryo develops a brain of unmistakable human proportions, eyes, ears, mouth, kidneys, liver etc., and seems to be large by ten thousand times of the zygote. By the 6-week, tiny fingers appear, followed by the toes; the eyes which appeared in simple form in the first month develops lens and retina; the eyelids start to take place, brain waves can be recorded by EEG (Electro-Encephalograph) and the ears continue to develop. By the seventh week, the baby has individual fingerprints, ear is present and the inner ear with its hearing and balancing mechanism is well established; skeleton is complete and he/she makes the first movement of body and newly grown limbs. At eight-week spontaneous movements of the embryo begins.

Since, the embryo witness rapid growth with appearance of all major organs of the body during embryonic stage, it is considered as the most critical stage of prenatal development. During this period the embryo is also susceptible to attack of virus '*rubella*' (German measles). In case the virus attacks, the babies are at high risk of being born blind and brain damaged. Proper environmental precautions and immunisation of the expectant mothers against rubella are proved significant in reducing probability of the disease.

FETAL PERIOD: FROM THE END OF EIGHT WEEKS TO BIRTH

The fetal stage starts at about the end of eight weeks and continues until birth. The organism is now called a 'fetus' since he/she is easily recognisable as human fetus. During this stage the sex organ is well developed to ascertain the gender of the baby. The organism undergoes astounding structural as well as functional changes. There is rapid increase in weight and length. The organs which appeared in the embryonic stage take their final shape, proportion, position in the body and start to function. This stage coincides with major developments in the nervous system including the brain, sensory development, and motor development.

Three months after fertilization the fetus is about 3 inches long and weighs about 3 ounces. The fetus now makes facial expressions and even smiles, sucks thumbs, can bend and close fingers and thumbs, open mouth in response to pressure applied at the base of the thumb.

By the end of fourth month of pregnancy the fetus is about 6 inches long and weighs about 4-7 ounces. The uterus expands and changes its shape to accommodate the growing baby, the pregnancy begins to show externally. The mother can feel, for the first time, arm, and leg movements. The inner ear of the fetus is completely developed and the baby hears sounds from outside world as well as from the mother's heart and digestive system and responds to light if shown on to the mother's abdomen.

By the end of the fifth month the baby is 12 inches long and weighs about a pound. The head of the embryo becomes just a quarter of its total size which is almost 50 % of its total size at two months of pregnancy. Head, hair, eyelashes, and nails are now growing. To protect the baby's skin from the amniotic fluid, a greasy substance called *vernix* covers the body. Between this stage and birth the baby gains weight and develops an insulating layer of fat beneath the skin. He or she also receives maternal antibodies against some infections as a temporary protection until the infant's own immune system is better developed. During the last three months, the fetus grows at about 8 ounces each week. By eight months, the fetus is virtually fully formed into a baby. However, premature birth during this period is associated with risk of perinatal and postnatal death out of breathing problems.

In this way a fertilized zygote implanted in mother's womb lands on earth after passing an average of 266-280 days. At birth typical length varies from 17 to 21 inches and average weight is 6 to 7 pounds.

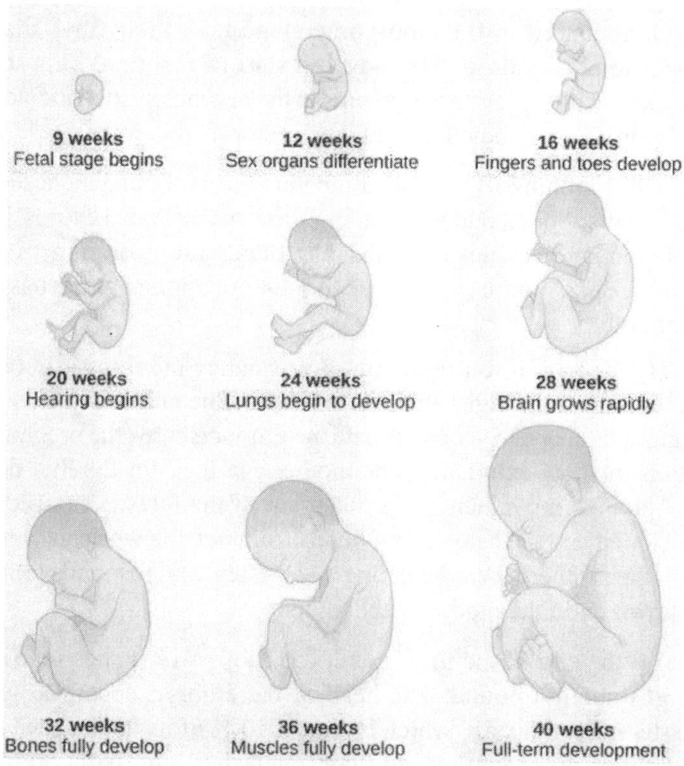

Figure: 7: Fetal Growth and Development. *Source*: http://oer@go.org

The course of development described above, lists the following features of prenatal development.

- The prenatal period is characterised by rapid growth and development. The growth rate is highest of all the stages in human life. It is so fast that a microscopically small cell, weighs about 7.5 pound and 20 inches long at birth.

- Growth during prenatal period occurs in two directions, cephalocaudal and proximodistal. It commences with the brain and head areas and then proceeds down the body (cephalocaudal); and starts from the midline and works its way outward (proximodistal).
- The heredity endowments are fixed at the time of conception. No environmental intervention can change it.
- The sex of the organism is fixed at the time of conception.
- The developing organism is a parasite during this period. It depends upon the mother for oxygen and other nourishment.
- The quality of environment available in mother's womb determines the quality of prenatal development.
- The organism is prone to developmental hazards ranging from mild birth defects to fatal or after birth death.
- The significant people develop attitude during prenatal period.

CONDITIONS AFFECTING PRENATAL DEVELOPMENT AND DEVELOPMENTAL HAZARDS

The course of human development (prenatal as well as postnatal) is influenced by two factors, *heredity* and *environment.* The role of heredity in developing organism is described in Chapter-5 showing how genetic factors determine the gender, observable traits, and other psycho-physical traits. The influence of genes and chromosomes in producing disorders and diseases are also detailed. In this section, the environmental and other parental factors determining prenatal development and its hazards are mapped.

In general, the 'environment' means all the factors available in our surrounding that influence human development after birth. But, in truth, the environment starts operating from the moment of conception. The environment available inside the mother's womb as well as outside during pregnancy, have intense impact on prenatal development with their lasting effect during and after birth. Favourable environment during pregnancy results in birth of normal and healthy babies whereas exposure to unfavourable environment, despite inheriting healthy genetic codes, may result in miscarriage or stillbirth and birth of babies with several types of birth defects. The conditions influencing prenatal development are discussed below.

Exposure to Teratogen

A teratogen is an agent which causes birth defects- physical, cognitive, or behavioural. Every developing organism is exposed to some or the other kinds of teratogen in varied magnitude across the prenatal development. The risk of complications of teratogens depends upon the dose and time of their exposure. Some of the complications arise during pregnancy, some at birth while some other complications appear long after birth. The common teratogens and their consequences are listed below.

***Maternal medications and drugs*:** Unsupervised use of medicines and drugs can have devastating effect on the fetus. Even the prescribed drugs sometimes have disastrous consequences. Many anti-depressant, antibiotics and hormone drugs can pass through the placenta and affect the developing offspring. Depending on the time and dose of exposure, abnormalities like prematurity, low weight birth, birth defects, asthma, brain damage and other anatomical defects of the new-born can appear. Damage during germinal period may even prevent implantation of the blastocyst to the uterine wall. The non-prescribed and over the counter drugs like high dose of aspirin (used to treat headache), diet pills can lead to maternal and fetal bleeding and growth impairment. Even the birth control pills taken well before conception can affect the brain development of the fetus. Therefore, the expectant mothers should avoid taking medicines unless prescribed by experienced medical professionals.

***Illicit drugs*:** The illicit drugs like marijuana, cocaine, heroin etc. are psychoactive and are used to change moods and state of consciousness. Use of these drugs by expectant mother can have devastating prenatal environmental affect. Prenatal exposure of marijuana restricts the oxygen supply to the fetus and causes damages like low intelligence, learning and memory defects of the child in later stages of life. Damages of cocaine exposure involves reduced birth weight, reduced length and head circumference, slower growth rate even after birth. Heroin has been associated with behavioural difficulties like withdrawal symptoms, irritability, disturbed sleep, impaired motor control etc.

Nicotine: Smoking and other forms of nicotine consumption during pregnancy adversely affects the growing organism during prenatal period, birth and during postnatal period. When an expectant mother smokes, the nicotine and other forms of toxins get mixed in the mother's blood stream and enter the fetus through the placenta. It also reduces the content of oxygen and increases carbon monoxide in the fetus. The damages due to nicotine include miscarriage, preterm birth, low birth weight, respiratory problems, fetal and neonatal death etc. Recently, nicotine is found to be associated with attention deficit hyperactivity disorder (ADHD) in offspring. Moreover, second-hand smoke (negative smoking) from father's cigarettes may also indirectly influence the expectant child. Therefore, the husband and other close relatives should avoid smoking during pregnancy.

Alcohol: Fetal Alcohol Effects (FAE), a disorder which is characterised by low intelligence, mental retardation, delayed growth, and facial abnormalities in the offspring, is the result of alcohol consumption by expectant mother during pregnancy. Few years ago, there was lack of evidence showing the adverse effects of mild to moderate level alcohol consumption during pregnancy. However, recent researches confirmed that even small quantity of regular alcohol consumption can adversely affect the normal growth of the offspring at later stages. It can severely affect the brain development and may result in lower intelligence, abnormal behavioural and psychological functioning.

Caffeine: Though caffeine intake seems to have no impact on preterm birth and birth weight, data shows that women taking lots of caffeine in the form of chocolate, cola drinks coffee etc. experience more miscarriage and birth defects.

Other Environmental Toxins: Prospective babies are subject to miscarriage and other birth defects if exposed to toxins available in mother's surroundings. Toxins contained in polluted air and water, pesticides, different sprays, air and body fresheners, cosmetics products etc. are harmful for the normal development of the fetus. If uncontrolled, it may lead to miscarriage, birth defects and even fetal death.

X-rays and Radiation: Exposure to excessive x-rays which emits harmful radiations may adversely affect the developing fetus. Damages may include birth defects and miscarriage or stillbirths. However, sonography which uses sound wave for screening purpose is not proved harmful for the fetus.

Maternal Age

The age of mothers during conception determines the health of prospective babies. Conception at a younger as well as older age is associated with a greater risk for a variety of pregnancy and birth complications. The best age for conception is 20s.

The reproductive system of women before 20s is not well developed to nourish babies. Some researchers also argue that young mothers are poor and less educated to deal with pregnancies, often making pregnancy stressful resulting in preterm birth. Women who become pregnant during adolescence experience abortion, miscarriage, premature deliveries, giving birth to low weight babies and perinatal deaths compared to women of child bearing ages. Kirchengast and Hartmann (2003) reported that mortality rate of infants born to teen mothers is double that for mothers in their 20s.

The risks of pregnancy complications are greater not only for younger mothers but for atypically older women as well. Generally, conception at the age of above 35 has potential consequences for both mothers' and childrens health. There is a decline in the conditions of reproductive system and the womens egg at older age. Reports claim that by the age of 42 years, 90% of women's egg is no longer normal (Cnattingius, Berendes and Forman, 1993; Gibbs, 2002). Decline in reproductive system of mothers at older age increases the possibility of premature birth of babies with low birth weight, which also increases the rate of perinatal deaths. Older mothers also have greater possibility of giving birth of babies with *down syndrome*, a non-curable mental retardation caused by genetic complications. As such, pregnant women of older age should mandatorily undergo screening for *down syndrome* during first and second trimester of pregnancy for early detection and intervention.

Maternal Health and Diseases

The physical and mental health of a mother during pregnancy is one of the significant factors of development. A healthy mother who maintains appropriate nutrition intake, regular exercise and healthy lifestyle maximizes the chances of giving birth of a healthy baby. In contrast, illness in mother can have devastating effect on her prospective child. Diseases and infections from mother can transmit to the fetus in different stages of prenatal development and can cause serious complications. During conception the blood supply of the mother and the fetus comes in proximity in the placenta. Though placenta works as a terminal exchange and restricts the undesirable materials from entering the fetus, sometimes it fails. As such, if the mother is affected by disease and infections, they transmit to the fetus. Rubella (German measles) is such a disease that can transmit to the fetus from the mother's blood stream during embryonic period which can cause prenatal defects in the organism like blindness, deafness, heart disease etc. Other disease that can be transmitted to the fetus include chicken pox, mumps, tuberculosis, malaria, syphilis, and herpes. The genital herpes transmits to fetus during delivery from the birth canal of the mother, if it is infected so. The result may include death or brain damage of the new-born. Syphilis, a sexually transmitted disease, causes its damage to the fetus four months or more after conception. The damage includes eye lesions (blindness) and skin lesions. HIV/AIDS can be transmitted to the fetus in three ways, during gestation across placenta, during delivery through contact with maternal blood and fluid and postpartum (after birth) through breast feeding. Recently diabetes has been added in the list that can transmit from mother to the fetus. Therefore, women who plans to have children should get themselves tested well in advance to determine whether they are immune to diseases. With advancement in medical sciences some life-threatening diseases can be restricted from their transmission to the fetus. For example, if treated with antiviral drugs during pregnancy, less than 5 percent infants born with HIV/AIDS even if the mothers are infected so. If the mother's birth canal is infected with genital herpes and detected close to delivery, a caesarean birth can prevent transmission of the disease to the fetus.

Maternal Diet and Nutrition

A developing organism inside womb receives nutrition and other essential minerals from the mother's blood stream through placenta. Balanced diet of the mother consisting of required intake of calories, proteins, vitamins, and other minerals are important for normal growth and development of the fetus. Malnourished mothers are at greater risk of pregnancy complications like miscarriage, premature birth, birth defects, low birth weight, neural problems like spin a bifida etc. The mother being overweight (obesity) before and during pregnancy also creates complications like maternal infertility, hypertensive disorder, diabetes and giving birth of overweight babies, fetal death, stillbirth etc. Diet enriched with folic acid, b-complex vitamins, iron etc. significantly reduces the risk of premature birth. Unfortunately, large number of pregnant women is deprived of balanced diet worldwide, more particularly in poor countries. According to UN report (2010), the number of people vulnerable to hunger in the globe is close to one billion. Restrictions in diets that bring hunger on such a massive scale affect millions of children born to women living in those conditions. Dietary supplements have the potential to reduce some of the adverse impact caused by poor diet.

Maternal Emotional States and Stress

Emotional state of an expectant mother can have a long run effect on the developing fetus. Emotional states and mood of the mother influences the developing organism in direct as well as indirect way. Experiencing intense fear, anxiety, depression, and stress by the mother triggers the releases of harmful hormones such as *epinephrine* and *acetylcholine* into her blood stream which pass through the placenta and enter the fetus blood. These hormones create complications for the offspring like prematurity and low weight birth. Taige and Others (2007) indicated that pregnant women with high level of stress are at increased risk of giving birth of child with emotional and cognitive problems, attention deficit hyperactivity disorder (ADHD) and language delay. More over, the expectant mother with high level depression, anxiety and stress may not take proper prenatal care which may harm the developing organism indirectly. The significant peoples like husband, parents and other family member should take proper care of the emotional state of the mother during pregnancy. In case of intense situation consultation with trained therapist should be sought to avoid negative consequences.

Incompatible Blood Types

Blood grouping is determined by surface structure of red blood cells which is decided by inherited genes. Blood is typed by ABO and by RH factor. The types of blood describe nothing but kinds of proteins present or absence in blood cells. As per the ABO, there are 4 main blood groups- A, B, O and AB. As per RH factor, blood is typed in to Rh-positive and Rh-negative. Rh-positive implies RH protein is present in blood cells whereas Rh-negative means absence of RH protein. When ABO and RH described together, there are eight different blood types- A+, A-, B+, B-, O+, O-, AB+ and AB-. Incompatibility occurs during pregnancy if mother is Rh-negative and the fetus is Rh-positive. In such cases the mother's body does not recognise the RH protein present in the fetus and consider it as a foreign substance. Eventually mother's immune system produces antibodies that attack the fetus. The resulting damage may include miscarriage, stillbirth, anaemia, jaundice, heart defects, brain damage or death soon after birth. However, the possibility of RH incompatibility is very less as most people are Rh-positive.

Attitude of Significant Peoples

Attitude of parents and other significant peoples are formed during prenatal period which indirectly influence the developing organism before and after birth. They serve the basis for prenatal as well as postnatal care towards the coming child. The factors determining attitude may be physical, psychological, and socio-cultural. If an expectant mother suffers from physical illness during pregnancy or have experience of physical complications during previous pregnancies may develop unfavourable attitude and see the current pregnancy as a burden. Psychological factors like desire to have children or not, desire for a particular gender, emotional stress, maternal aspirations, dreams, and fantasies etc. play significant role in forming attitude of parents towards the child. If unexpected conception occurs and the parents donot want parenthood at the time, they may develop a negative attitude which may adversely influence child care and rearing methods. In contrast, who aspire to be good parents have more favourable attitude towards pregnancy. Socio-cultural factors include socio-economic status of the family, influence of relatives and friends, influence of mass-media etc. If the family belongs to poor socio-economic class, parents may treat the pregnancy as burden, while upper class will treat it as fulfilment of marriage. Similarly, if friends and other relatives are unhappy of their parenthood and constantly complains of it, the parents-to-be may develop unfavourable attitude towards their to-be-child and in turn seem it as frustrating and annoying.

Besides parents, other significant people like grandparents, aunts, uncles, siblings also develop attitude towards the to-be-child during this period which is crucial in child development. A favourable attitude of significant peoples can go a long way in fostering normal growth and development of the offspring before and after birth.

MEASURES TO REDUCE HAZARDS AND OPTIMIZE PRENATAL DEVELOPMENT

As there is no control over the developmental hazards caused by genetic factors, efforts should be directed to optimize environmental conditions to foster smooth development. A couple may take care of the following points before and after conception for reducing risks of prenatal developmental hazards.

- First, the couple should decide whether they really want to be parent or not. It should be decided by husband and wife together. The decision should not be influenced by interpersonal pressure in anyway. Else, unfavourable attitude will be formed towards parenthood and to-be-child, which is very crucial. Considerably, pregnancies should be ensured during 20 to 30 years of age of women.
- Once they are psychologically prepared for parenthood, the couple should ensure their physical fitness. A visit should be made to physician for screening of certain diseases and to ascertain whether they are fertile or not. Some cases of infertility in both male and female can be corrected while others are not. Other potential medical issues, if any, should be fixed.
- Contraceptive pills should be avoided well before getting pregnant as it may create brain damage to the developing fetus. In case of obesity, weight should be reduced considerably to avoid possible hazards. Vaccination against rubella (German measles) should be taken at least three months prior of getting pregnant. Proper amount of nutrients including folic acid, iron, and proteins should be taken even before conception.
- After conception, regular visit should be made to the medical practitioner. Balanced diet involving all required nutrients should be consumed in adequate quantity. Dietary supplements of vitamins like folic acid, iron, calcium, protein, and other necessary minerals to be taken regularly

as per the physician's advice. Caffeine intake should be monitored. Maintaining a healthy lifestyle, regular exercise, adequate rest, and sleep fosters prenatal development.

- The first trimester is most critical as all the major organs of the embryo starts forming and the embryo becomes a miniature human being. Possibility of miscarriage is highest during this stage. As such, precautions in terms of diet, physical rest, and emotional stability should be ensured.
- Should avoid use of any non-prescribed drugs. Drugs should be used only in unavoidable situation as directed by the physician. Also, should avoid consuming psychoactive and sedative drugs like heroin, cocaine, marijuana etc.
- Alcohol and nicotine consumption needs to be avoided. The husband should also be encouraged to quit smoking, if so, to prevent adverse effect of negative smoking of the expectant mother.
- Should avoid exposure to radiation and other forms of toxins at work place and surroundings.
- During the end of first trimester, screening for down syndrome and other genetic disorders should be done. If the expectant mother is above 35 years of age or there is any history of down syndrome in the family of any of the partners, screening is a must. During second trimester anomaly scan should be performed to detect any anatomical defects in the fetus. However, should not undergo excessive scan to see the developing fetus out of excitement, which often couples do.
- The partner and other family members should take care of the emotional state of the expectant mother. In case of chronic stress, depression, and anxiety, help from therapist should be sought.
- Research studies deny the benefit of complete bed rest during pregnancy. Hence, movements and exercise to be

encouraged. However, strong physical labours, climbing staircase, lifting weights, exposure to vulnerable objects etc. should be avoided.

- Finally, forms of birth-whether natural, caesarean, or any other, should be decided considering the health conditions of the expectant mother and the to-be-child. For example, natural birth must be avoided in case the expectant mother is affected by genital herpes and HIV/AIDS. The genital herpes transmits to fetus during delivery from the birth canal of the mother, if it is infected so. The result may cause death or brain damage of the new-born. Similarly, HIV/AIDS can be transmitted to fetus during delivery through contact with maternal blood and fluid.

THE BIRTH PROCESS

Birth is a short break in the process of development to a life which started nine months before right at conception. It is only a transition from prenatal to post-natal environment. After spending a period of 40 weeks of sheltered environment in the mother's uterus, the fetus comes into the larger world. It is after that the parasite organism becomes independent and survives on his/her own biological system. Early philosophers, scientists and psychologists viewed birth as traumatic and studies on birth were mostly concentrated on finding ways to reduce birth pain for the mother and to ensure safety of the mother-child duo during and after birth. The effects of birth process in postnatal developments, state of developments present at birth and their after-effects were somehow overlooked. Since development is continuous, it is apparent that birth, like conception and prenatal stage, triggers later developments. In fact, birth is an event of tremendous importance form medical, psychological, and social perspectives.

Natural Birth

The process of birth initiates normally from 38-40 weeks of prenatal development. The natural child birth is spontaneous and requires little or no outside interference. This is most practised birthing procedure practised till few decades ago. In natural birth the baby emerges through mother's vaginal canal. The head of the baby emerges first, followed by shoulder and then other body parts. Yet in some cases, the buttocks emerge first, while in others the baby lie crosswise in the uterus just before birth. Delivery of such babies requires instrumental assistance or C-section which are discussed later.

The natural birth process generally consists of three stages. The first stage starts with the mild uterine contractions to cervix and ends with opening of the cervix, the neck of the uterus, to allow the baby to pass through. At the beginning of the labour, mother's body releases hormonal signals including *oxytocin* from pituitary gland that prompts uterine muscle fibres to contract with the cervix to make it stretch and open. Initially, the contractions are mild (known as *Braxton-Hicks contractions*) and occur around every 10 to 15 minutes and last for about 30 seconds. Gradually contractions become stronger and occur around 3 to 5 minutes of interval and lasts for about 45 seconds. Eventually, the contractions increase their intensity, pushing the baby towards the cervix. As a result, the cervix dilates and expands enough to allow the baby passage. This is the longest stage of labour, duration of which varies depending on mother's age, race, ethnicity, number of prior pregnancies and other factors. Typically, this stage takes 6 to 12 hours for firstborn children.

The second stage of natural birth begins when the baby's head starts to move through the cervix and birth canal and lasts until the baby completely left mother's body, which require about 20 to 60 minutes. During this stage, contractions occur after every 2 to 3 minutes and lasts for about 60 seconds. With each contraction the baby comes out of the birth canal, emerging the head first. These contractions are also aided by pushes by mother's abdominal muscles. The second stage completes as the baby completely emerges out of the mother's body.

The third stage of labour starts after the baby is delivered. It includes the delivery of placenta, umbilical cord and other membranes that nourishes the baby inside the womb. This is the shortest stage of birth process which lasts only for minutes.

Today, most natural child birth uses at least some medications. Generally, medications are used either to reduce birth pain for the to-be-mother and/or to induce labour. *Analgesia* like tranquilizers, narcotics etc. are used to reduce pain. Sometimes labour is artificially induced by using *Oxytocin* which stimulates uterine contractions to enable cervix opening. Other techniques like breathing and muscle exercises are often taught to mothers' who planned a natural birth to reduce birth pain.

Assisted Vaginal Birth

Vaginal delivery that adopts instrumental help is called assisted vaginal birth. The need of assistance may be different considering the health conditions of the mother and the baby. Conditions like baby's weight and size, position of the baby in the uterus, size of the pelvis etc. are considered before deciding assisted vaginal birth. For example, if the fetus is too large to emerge through the birth canal, *episiotomy*, an incision between birth canal and anus of the mother, is done to enable easy emergence through the birth canal.

Two types of assisted vaginal delivery are mostly performed- *Vacuum extraction* and *Forceps delivery*. In *vacuum extraction*, a suction cup with attached handle is placed in the vagina and applied to the top of the baby's head to help guide the baby out of the birth canal. In *Forceps delivery,* forceps (instruments look like two large spoons) is inserted into the vagina and placed around the baby's head. Gentle traction is applied through the forceps to guide the baby come out of the birth canal. The advantage of assisted vaginal deliveries is that it eliminates caesarean delivery that requires major operative procedure.

Caesarean (C-Section) Birth

In normal cases the head of the baby emerges out of the birth canal first. If it is not so and the fetus emerges in *breech* position (buttocks appear first instead of head) or in *transverse* position (fetus lie crosswise in the uterus), several complications ranging from mild birth defects to death may occur. For example, the umbilical cord may get compressed and the baby may face oxygen deficiency or excessive labour pressure may result in brain damage. In such cases, caesarean section is initiated. In caesarean birth the baby is removed from the uterus through an incision in mother's abdomen.

Though caesarean delivery is advisable in unavoidable conditions, it has become a regular practice in present times. Socio-economic and psychological reasons are associated with it. Even most mothers and family members themselves opt for caesarean birth over natural delivery to skip its pain and trauma. However, the benefits and risks of caesarean delivery are being debated.

EVALUATING BABY'S HEALTH SOON AFTER BIRTH: THE APGAR SCALE

As the birth process completes, the foetus is no longer attached to the mother's body. The new-born is now responsible for its own survival. The atmosphere totally changes for the new-born when it comes outside the womb. Various conditions and complications may appear in this period. The foetus is now supposed to be a fully functional human being. For this, it becomes necessary for the new-born to show certain signs shortly after birth to confirm its health. Certain inspections are conducted to check whether the new-born is capable to human functioning or not. Some common inspections like checking number of fingers can be done by parents themselves but, expert health professional uses standard assessment techniques among which the Apgar Scale is found to be most preferable.

The Apgar Scale is a standardised measurement scale developed by physician Dr. Virginia Apgar, which assesses the viability and fitness of the new born baby right after the delivery. This scale reports the overall health of the neonate and is performed upon 5 major components or criteria that represents its name APGAR. These are namely, appearance or colour, pulse or heart rate, grimace response or reflexes, activity or muscle tone and respiration or breathing rate.

The assessment is to be administered upon every new-born and he/she must go through each of these components two times, firstly at a 1-minute mark and secondly at a 5-minutes mark. The scale is developed under the score of 0, 1 and 2. The obtained score shows whether the new-born is alright or he/she needs some additional medical assistance besides the usual. If the neonate shows a low score, it indicates that he/she requires special medical attention.

The overall Apgar score is calculated by adding all the number of points the neonate secures at each category. The highest score might be 10 and the lowest score might be 0. The average score is considered to be 7, that means if the new-born scores 7 or above then it indicates a good health and if it scores lower than that, the infant may require additional care and medication. This score should be shown twice, both at 1 minute mark and 5 minutes mark. If the score is lower than 7 at 1-minute mark, it should improve at the 5-minute mark. And if it does not improve, then immediate medical care or resuscitation can be applied. However, a lower score does not always imply any serious medical condition that may remain in later life.

Thus, the Apgar scale is considered to be a convenient and reliable standardised method for addressing the status of the overall health of the neonate right after the birth and also suggests special immediate measures if the infant responds negatively. It also provides the new parents with knowledge and future awareness for the good heath of their child.

Bibliography

Allmark, P. (2002). The ethics of research with children (Ethical issues in research). *Nurse Researcher, 10*(2), 7-20.

Archer, J. (1992). *Ethology and human development*. Rowman & Littlefield.

Baltes, P. B., & Goulet, L. R. (1970). Status and issues of a life-span developmental psychology. *Life-span Developmental Psychology*, 3-21.

Baltes, P. B., Reese, H. W., & Lipsitt, L. P. (1980). Life-span developmental psychology. *Annual Review of Psychology, 31*(1), 65-110.

Baron, R. A., & Misra, G. (2002). *Psychology-Indian subcontinent edition* (5th ed.). Pearson.

Bogin, B. (2020). *Patterns of human growth* (Vol. 88). Cambridge University Press.

Cairns, R. B. (1998). The making of developmental psychology.

Cameron, N., & Schell, L. (Eds.). (2021). *Human growth and development*. Academic Press.

Chand, T. (1993). *Modern child psychology*. Anmol Publications.

Chaube, S. P. (2004). *Abnormal psychology* (3rd ed.). Lakshmi Narain Agarwal Educational Publishers.

Cole, L., & Hall, I. N. (1969). *Psychology of adolescence* (7th ed.). Holt, Rinehart and Winston, Inc.

Cnattingius, S. V. E. N., Berendes, H. W., & Forman, M. R. (1993).

Do delayed child bearers face increased risks of adverse pregnancy outcomes after the first birth? *Obstetrics and Gynecology*, *81*(4), 512-516.

Crandell, T. L., Crandell, C. H., & Zandeen, J. W. (2012). *Human development* (9th ed.). McGraw Hill Education (India) Private Limited.

Deary, I. J., Johnson, W., & Houlihan, L. M. (2009). Genetic foundations of human intelligence. *Human Genetics*, *126*(1), 215-232.

Feldman, R. S. (2015). *Development across the life-span* (7th ed.). Doling Kindersley Pvt. Ltd. (Indian Edition).

Flavell, J. H. (1963). The developmental psychology of Jean Piaget.

Gibbs, N., Horowitz, J. M., & Rawe, J. (2002). Making time for a baby. *Time*, *159*(15), 48-53.

Goodenough, F. L., & Anderson, J. E. (1931). Experimental child study.

Goodman, G., Ripps, H., & Siegel, I. M. (1965). Sex-linked ocular disorders: Trait expressivity in males and carrier females. *Archives of Ophthalmology*, *73*(3), 387-398.

Goswamee, G. (2008). *Child development and child care*. Arun Prakashan.

Gottlieb, G. (1976). Conceptions of prenatal development: Behavioural embryology. *Psychological Review*, *83*(3), 215.

Goulet, L. R., & Baltes, P. B. (Eds.). (2013). *Life-span developmental psychology: Research and theory*. Academic Press.

Graue, M. E., & Walsh, D. J. (1998). *Studying children in context: Theories, methods, and ethics*. Sage.

Greene, S., & Hogan, D. (Eds.). (2005). *Researching children's experience: Approaches and methods*. Sage. Harris, M., & Butterworth, G. (2002). *Developmental Psychology- A student's handbook*. Psychology Press, Taylor & Francis Group.

Hill, M. (2005). Ethical considerations in researching children's experiences. *Researching Children's Experience*, 61-86.

Hurlock, E. B. (1976). *Developmental psychology* (4th ed.). Tata McGraw Hill Publishing Company Limited.

Hurlock, E. B. (1978). *Child growth and development* (5th ed.). Tata McGraw-Hill Publishing Company Ltd.

Hurlock, E. B. (1981). *Developmental psychology- A life-span approach* (5th ed.). McGraw Hill Education (India) Private Limited.

Hurlock, E. B. (1997). *Child development* (6th ed.). Tata McGraw Hill Education Private Limited.

Lidral, A. C., & Murray, J. C. (2004). Genetic approaches to identify disease genes for birth defects with cleft lip/palate as a model. *Birth Defects Research Part A: Clinical and Molecular Teratology*, *70*(12), 893-901.

Lindblad, F., & Hjern, A. (2010). ADHD after fetal exposure to maternal smoking. *Nicotine & Tobacco Research*, *12*(4), 408-415.

Lu, M. C., & Lu, J. S. (2008). Prenatal care. In M. M. Haith & J. B. Benson (Eds.), *Encyclopaedia of Infancy and Early Childhood Development*. Elsevier.

Kale, S. V. (2000). *Child psychology and child guidance* (6th ed.). Himalaya Publishing House.

Kelly, G. A. (1955). *The psychology of personal constructs*. New York: Norton.

Kirchengast, S., & Hartmann, B. (2003). Impact of maternal age and maternal somatic characteristics on newborn size. *American Journal of Human Biology*, *15*(2), 220-228.

Mader, S. S. (2011). *Inquiry into life* (13th ed.). McGraw-Hill.

Mangal, S. K. (1987). *Abnormal psychology.* Sterling Publishers Private Limited.

Mangal, S. K. (2002). *Advanced educational psychology* (2nd ed.). Prentice-Hall of India.

Mangal, S. K. (2015). *Educating exceptional children: An introduction to special education.*Prentice-Hall of India.

Maraldi, C., Harris, T. B., Newman, A. B., Kritchevsky, S. B., Pahor, M., Koster, A., ... & Health ABC Study. (2009). Moderate alcohol intake and risk of functional decline: The Health, aging, and body composition study. *Journal of the American Geriatrics Society*, *57*(10), 1767-1775.

Martínez-Galiano, J. M., Hernández-Martínez, A., Rodríguez-Almagro, J., & Delgado-Rodríguez, M. (2019). Quality of life of women after giving birth: Associated factors related with the birth process. *Journal of Clinical Medicine*, *8*(3), 324.

Matthews, D. J., Subotnik, R. F., & Horowitz, F. D. (2009). A developmental perspective on giftedness and talent: Implications for research, policy, and practice.

McCall, R. B. (1977). Challenges to a science of developmental psychology. *Child Development*, 333-344.

McCammon, R. W. (1970). Human growth and development. *Human Growth and Development.*

McDonald, S. D., Han, Z., Mulla, S., Murphy, K. E., Beyene, J., & Ohlsson, A. (2009). Preterm birth and low birth weight among in vitro fertilization singletons: A systematic review and meta-analyses. *European Journal of Obstetrics & Gynecology and Reproductive Biology*, *146*(2), 138-148.

McDonald, S. D., Han, Z., Mulla, S., Ohlsson, A., Beyene, J., & Murphy, K. E. (2010). Preterm birth and low birth weight among in vitro fertilization twins: A systematic review and meta-analyses. *European Journal of Obstetrics & Gynecology and Reproductive Biology*, *148*(2), 105-113.

Moise, K. J. (2005). Fetal RhD typing with free DNA in maternal plasma. *American Journal of Obstetrics & Gynecology*, *192*(3), 663-665.

Nadel, L. (2003). Down's syndrome: A genetic disorder in bio-behavioural perspective. *Genes, Brain and Behaviour*, *2*(3), 156-166.

National Down Syndrome Society (NDSS). (2007). *Parent and professional information*. www.ndss.org/information/general_info.html

Nesselroade, J. R., & Reese, H. W. (Eds.). (2013). *Life-span developmental psychology: Methodological issues*. Academic Press.

Norman, J. E., Mackenzie, F., Owen, P., Mactier, H., Hanretty, K., Cooper, S., ... & Norrie, J. (2009). Progesterone for the prevention of preterm birth in twin pregnancy (STOPPIT): A randomised, double-blind, placebo-controlled study and meta-analysis. *The Lancet*, *373*(9680), 2034-2040.

Overton, W. F. (1998). Developmental psychology: Philosophy, concepts, and methodology.

Richardson, K. (2005). *Developmental psychology: How nature and nurture interact*. Psychology Press.

Samson, L. F. (1988). Perinatal viral infections and neonates. *The Journal of Perinatal & Neonatal Nursing*, *1*(4), 56-65.

Santrock, J. W. (2010). *Life-span development* (13th ed.). McGraw Hill Education (India) Private Limited.

Sarason, I. G (1976). *Abnormal psychology* (2nd ed.). Prentice-Hall, Inc.

Sharma, R. N., & Sharma, R. (2017). *Child psychology*. Atlantic Publishers & Distributors (P) Ltd.

Sigelman, C. K., & Rider, E. A. (2014). *Life-span human development*. Cengage Learning.

Skinner, C. E. (1977). *Educational psychology* (4th ed.). Prentice-Hall of India Private Limited.

Slater, A. E., & Bremner, G. E. (2003). *An introduction to developmental psychology*. Blackwell Publishing.

Starr, C., Evers, C. & Starr, L. (2010). *Biology today and tomorrow with physiology* (3rd ed.). Cengage Learning.

Staudinger, U. M., & Gluck, J. (2011). Psychological wisdom research. *Annual Review of Psychology, 62*. Palo Alto, CA: Annual Reviews.

Steel, A. J., & Sutcliffe, A. (2009). Long-term health implications for children conceived by IVF/ICSI. *Human Fertility*, *12*(1), 21-27.

Strange, J. R. (1965). *Abnormal psychology: Understanding behaviour disorders*. Tata McGraw-Hill Publishing Company Limited.

Talge, N. M., Neal, C., Glover, V., & Early Stress, Translational Research and Prevention Science Network: Fetal and Neonatal Experience on Child and Adolescent Mental Health. (2007). Antenatal maternal stress and longterm effects on child neurodevelopment: how and why?. *Journal of Child Psychology and Psychiatry*, *48*(34), 245-261.

Thakur, A. S., & Berwal, S. (2010). *Development of learner and teaching-learning process*. Agarwal Publications.

Thapar, A., Fowler, T., Rice, F., Scourfield, J., Van Den Bree, M., Thomas, H., ... & Hay, D. (2003). Maternal smoking during pregnancy and attention deficit hyperactivity disorder symptoms in offspring. *American Journal of Psychiatry*, *160*(11), 1985-1989.

United Nations (UN). (2010). *The millennium development goals report 2010*. United Nations.

Woodhead, M. (1999). Reconstructing developmental psychology—Some first steps. *Children & Society*, *13*(1), 3-19.

www.srcd.org

www.invtra.com

www.colorbox.com

www.healthtree.com

www.ashg.com

www.youtube.com

www.downsyndrome.in

http://oer@go.org

Index